Bright Ideas
Word Games

Written by Martin Coles

Contents

Published by Scholastic Publications Ltd,
Marlborough House, Holly Walk,
Leamington Spa, Warwickshire CV32 4LS.

© 1989 Scholastic Publications Ltd

Written by Martin Coles
Edited by Jackie Cunningham-Craig
Sub-edited by Jane Morgan
Illustrations by Gay Galsworthy

Printed in Great Britain by
Loxley Brothers Ltd, Sheffield

ISBN 0 590 76204 4

Front and back cover: designed by Sue Limb.

Introduction

This book contains practical ideas for simple language games which can be promoted with individual children, groups, or classes and which are intended to engage children and set them free to enjoy language learning based on play and humour.

Of course, language teaching at its best does not ask children to deal with language out of context. For various good reasons most teachers have now abandoned the attempt to increase competence in language through direct instruction as this used to be represented in exercises testing grammar. A long series of studies of primary classrooms, however, has revealed that opportunities for the creative use of language are still significantly fewer than for formal comprehension and spelling work.[1] Yet to learn new language, children need a great variety of stimuli and they need to meet language in a great many different contexts. The activities in this book provide one set of such contexts. They generate language and make new linguistic demands on participants, increasing the range and variety of language work. In this way *Bright Ideas Word Games* takes up the suggestion of a recent government report on the 'Teaching of English Language' that 'Children should practise writing in a variety of forms . . .' because 'the activity gives them the opportunity to experiment with language'.[2]

Games-related language activities do not ask children to handle language divorced from their real world since, as the 'Kingman Report' points out, word-play is one of the ways in which we use language: 'People in general are curious about the workings of language, and English lessons should build on that curiosity. Children in particular are fascinated by word games — by puns, backslang, tongue-twisters, conundrums, double meanings, anagrams, palindromes, etymologies and "secret" languages'.[3]

Childhood particularly is a time of play, with language as with much else. Children's rhymes and riddles and word-play games are preserved, sometimes across the centuries. Joke fashions arise spontaneously among children and gain currency. Evidence of children playing with meaning and ideas, with language and conventions and taboos, with rhythms and sounds, can be gathered from any playground. Yet the idea that word-play is a fundamental part of children's development as language users, is often not acknowledged as a valuable constituent of the primary school curriculum. The activities in this book offer the chance to engage with these areas of language. For example, the second chapter 'Sending messages' contains activities which require children to invent 'secret' languages.

In word-play there is usually an element of humour and/or a sense of the absurd. It is present in much literature. Children's magazines, comics and 'Annuals' use this element extensively to gain popularity. Teachers can exploit the vitality and importance of this aspect of language so that it becomes a part of a fertile classroom language environment. If we are concerned to stimulate children's imaginative energies sufficiently for them to extend and develop their creativity in language, then why not allow the creative process to feed on the unusual and bizarre as well as the rational and ordered? Given such encouragement children will begin to build and employ a greater range of language resources.

Play with words invigorates language, but there are also other gains to be made from word games. They have a major part to play in developing confidence in language, which they do by providing psychological security at the same time as psychological freedom. This freedom and security arises from, on the one hand, the discipline imposed by the boundaries of the specific activity, and on the other, freedom to think creatively within those boundaries. The child is freed from the burden of having to pay attention to spelling, grammar, punctuation, handwriting and content all at once and can concentrate on one aspect of language only. Without the worry that inexperience will be mistaken for stupidity and without the threat of correction by an adult, much can go on which is experimental and open to revision and expansion by the pupils themselves. Word games have a liberating force. They help build confidence by allowing children to feel that they have power over words, that they can devise and revise, and that it pays to take risks with language.

These activities can lead also to knowledge about language. To say that a skilful teacher will see opportunities here for using a particular activity to impart some formal language knowledge is not to advocate knowledge about language for the sake of knowledge, nor to suggest that such knowledge should be taught in some linear, textbook way. Nevertheless the implicit knowledge about language which pupils will gain from these activities can be made explicit through discussion, if the teacher feels that it is appropriate. The 'Kingman Report' explains how this might happen. 'If a move from spontaneous

practice to considered reflection is sensitively handled by the teacher, it becomes quite natural to talk about language in classrooms'.[4]

For instance, some activities in this book ask children to explore sentence construction. Here the activity itself, if supported by discussion, will draw attention to the structural properties that sentences have in common. The teacher might, for example, lead the discussion towards the fact that verbs function as the nucleus of a sentence, and explain that pupils can check for themselves the presence of verbs in sentences in their other writing. This might be one way of moving towards the attainment target in the National Curriculum which expects that at level three children will be able to 'Show a growing awareness of word families and their relationships'.[5] Obviously this is an area where teachers

need to use their professional judgement. An understanding of descriptive technical language is not needed to enjoy the activities, but can certainly be introduced if, on occasions, teachers judge it appropriate, for example, to introduce children to words such as homophone, synonym and onomatopoeia.

Teachers may have other specific purposes in mind when using this material. Children might be encouraged to widen their written vocabulary by a realisation that they have more words to call on than they normally use. Some games will give the opportunity to put down on paper for the first time words that they may have in their spoken vocabulary but are unsure how to spell and therefore would not normally write. It is easy for adults to forget that children sometimes find new words awkward to handle. Activities which allow pupils to play with words can help

overcome this awkwardness. So the 'Kingman Report' suggestion that 'Both professional poets and tentative beginners can be led to felicitous discoveries of new words and phrases (and even thoughts) by the exigencies of rhyme'[6] is taken up by games which require children to invent rhymes and thereby discover new words.

There are activities here which provide children with chances to learn techniques of the sort writers employ to help convey what they want to say succinctly or dramatically or in rhyme, or in many other ways. All these things help children towards satisfaction with the way they use language.

Of course there can be disadvantages in the use of games in school. If used injudiciously there can be too little sense of order and structure in a child's learning. But, these activities are not meant to be the sole content of a child's language learning in the classroom. Nor are they offered as a systematic and finely-graded programme. They offer an additional teaching dimension, for occasional use, and should not become occupational, like old-fashioned exercises, so that they become a chore.

Many of the activities will work best with small groups of children. Group talk seems the natural way to become involved in the games-related style of these activities, and if children work collaboratively they can, to some extent, resolve the problem that all writers have, of being cut off from the stimulus and corrective of listeners. But group work is not essential and some teachers will prefer to work in other ways.

All of the activities contained here have been tried out with classes either by the author or by other teachers. Nevertheless, in some circumstances, they will need adaptation. This is meant to be a practical book, but it should not therefore be used

children's ability to use words more confidently in order to communicate, celebrate, investigate and do all the range of things possible in their own extended writing.

All teachers know the child who sits hunched over his writing book, tongue over bottom lip, brow furrowed. Above all, the activities here are an attempt to say to that child especially, 'Sit up. Smile. Language is fun'.

REFERENCES

1   For example, *Education Observed 2: A review of published reports by HM Inspectors on primary schools and 11–16 and 12–16 comprehensive schools* (DES 1984) reports that 'Once children are competent writers the range and variety of their written work are often too restricted: older children in particular spend far too much of their time on undemanding and unprofitable comprehension and grammatical exercises . . . . Standards of written work are highest in those schools in which a wide range of written assignments is expected and carried out.' (p2)

2   *Report of the Committee of Inquiry into the Teaching of English Language* (The Kingman Report) HMSO 1988 (p10)

3   Ibid. (p13)

4   Ibid. (p13)

5   *English 5–11 in the National Curriculum* National Curriculum Council 1989 (p37)

6   *Report of the Committee of Inquiry into the Teaching of English Language* (The Kingman Report) HMSO 1988 (p38)

blindly. Even though an indication is given of the age at which it is thought each activity can most appropriately be introduced, it would be foolish to suggest that the ideas will all work equally well with children of differing abilities of that age. Teachers will need to use their characteristic energy and creativity to select from the book what they feel able to use and then adapt and develop the idea. They should feel free to take any idea and change it, re-organise it, combine it, distort it, or modify it. By doing this they should be able to offer individuals an element of enjoyable 'challenge' which is infinitely variable in the degree of that challenge, as opposed to offering standard activities irrespective of individual differences. You will know that children are enjoying playing with language and developing their own interests in it, when pupils themselves invent variants of the games and new approaches to the activities. Indeed it is hoped that children who involve themselves in these sorts of activities will become used to the fact that classroom language does not have to be teacher-initiated and teacher-directed. It is hoped too that they will be encouraged to indulge in a lot of private exploratory language, perhaps swapping notes in the lunch hour, writing poems on holiday, or devising a word game at home.

A steady diet of word games will not in itself ensure a worthwhile writing experience for primary school children. What the occasional word game activity can do is to encourage a lively interest in the tools of the trade and help to develop

Playing with words

Commercial word games of all sorts such as Scrabble and Word Mastermind will be enjoyed in many primary classrooms, but there are many other games, based around single words, that can be used to let children play with language. Many of the games in this section encourage children to look at words and find letter strings. Since the secret of learning to spell is to build an awareness of letter patterns, these games will help children to improve their spelling by leading towards an understanding of the probability of certain letters occurring in sequence. Other games carry different bonuses. For example, some offer opportunities for children to practice finding their way around a dictionary, others are designed to help young children practice visual discrimination of the kind they will need as they begin to read. However the prime purpose of all the games should be to encourage enjoyment of language.

Anagrams

Age range
Seven to eleven.

Group size
Whole class.

What you need
Pencil and paper.

What to do
An anagram is a word, or a phrase, formed by using the letters of a different word and changing the order. For example, 'shore' is an anagram of 'horse', and 'plum' is an anagram of 'lump'.

Ask half the class to devise anagrams for the other half to solve. Alternatively provide a list of anagrams on a certain theme for groups of children to solve. As the words and phrases get longer and the children become more ambitious it may be that clues are needed to solve the anagrams. For instance:

Anagram: hire tent
Clue: a number
Answer: thirteen.

Add a letter anagrams

Age range
Seven to eleven.

Group size
Pairs or groups.

What you need
Pencil and paper.

What to do
In pairs or groups, get one child to write a three letter word and then the others have to use those three letters plus one more to make a different word. Another letter is then added to the second word and the letters rearranged to make a five letter word. For example:

Starter word = Mat

Turn 1 : Mat + e = Team
Turn 2 : Team + s = Meats
Turn 3 : Meats + r = Master
Turn 4 : Master + m = Stammer

Starter word = Pit

Turn 1 : Pit + s = Pits
Turn 2 : Pits + l = Split
Turn 3 : Spilt + n = Splint

Starter word = Far

Turn 1 : Far + t = Raft
Turn 2 : Raft + c = Craft
Turn 3 : Craft + f + i = Traffic

Starter word = it

Turn 1 : It + h = Hit
Turn 2 : Hit + s = This
Turn 3 : This + g = Sight
Turn 4 : Sight + l = Slight

Rollagrams

Age range
Seven to eleven.

Group size
Small groups.

What you need
Six dice, sticky paper, egg-timer, pencil and paper.

What to do
For this game, you will need dice with letters on them. You can make these by putting small squares or circles of sticky paper over the numbers on ordinary dice and writing a letter on each side. The number of dice can vary, but six is perhaps the best. Players take it in turn to roll the dice and the rest of the group try, individually, to make a word from the letters rolled. Each word scores one point, so a player could score a number of points on one roll of the dice.

Alternatively the longest word scores one point, so if anyone makes a six-letter word they are sure of a point for that 'turn'. Use an egg-timer when the dice are rolled to determine how long players get to 'find' words. The game can, of course, be played as a co-operative activity.

Daft definitions

Age range
Nine to eleven.

Group size
Small groups.

What you need
Pencil and paper.

What to do
Daft definitions is a simple game in which the players have to make up new meanings for everyday words. The words can be provided so that players can compare definitions, or players can be asked to find their own words and offer daft definitions of them. For example:

Delight: when the electricity fails.
Revolt: when the electricity comes on again.

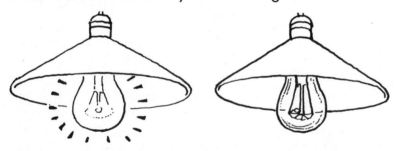

Capsize: a head measurement.

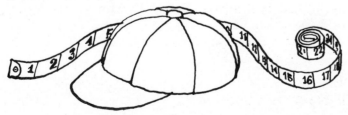

Pigmy: a pet swine.

Physics: the study of lemonade.

Dispel: to undo a wizard's magic.

Buttercup: a margarine dish.
Inspire: the area inside a church tower.
Norfolk: a term for people who never say 'yes' to anything.

Joke names

Age range
Nine to eleven.

Group size
Whole class.

What you need
Pencil and paper.

What to do
Get the children to make up joke family names. Have you heard of Mr and Mrs Chief and their very naughty daugher Miss Chief? Do you know the family who own the greengrocers shop, Mr and Mrs Ato and their son Tom Ato?

Can your class write a party guest list, including as many joke names as possible? Perhaps you would invite Mr and Mrs Croscope, the scientists, and their son Mike Croscope. And what about Mike's spotlessy clean relative Auntie Septic?

Variations
Ask your class to do the same thing with book titles. Have you read the book *The Millionaire* by Ivor Mint? Has your bookshop got *How to be an Optician* by Major Blind; or *The Case of The Oriental Lawnmower* by Miss Sing Toh? If your class can invent enough of these you could cover a set of books with plain paper jackets, ask children to write their invented titles and names on the spines and make a display shelf of books by joke authors.

Another variation on this activity is to ask the children to write a phrase or short sentence to describe a character with a humorous name. For example:

Josephine Juice squeezed herself into her tight clothes.

Michael Moon would only go out at night.

Enid Icicle looked at me with a frozen smile.

You could also get the children to match names to occupations and hobbies. For example:

Annie Mate is a cartoonist.

Mr X Pyred is an undertaker.

Sandy Beech is a lifeguard.

Polly Titian is an MP.

Will Steele is a burglar.

13

Patterns with words

Age range
Seven to eleven.

Group size
Pairs or small groups.

What you need
Pencil and paper.

What to do
Get the children to make a word chain with the last letter of one word acting as the first letter of the next. The children will find it easier, and more interesting, if the word chain is drawn as a set of steps. An element of competition can be added if groups or pairs of children compete against each other to produce the longest staircase (without using a dictionary).

This game can be made more thought provoking and used to reinforce vocabulary, perhaps to do with a current class topic, if it is stipulated that the words in the staircase must relate to a theme.

Variation 1
Ask the children to try to make a word chain using the last two letters of each word. For example:
    tap/ape/pet/ethnic/icon/onyx.
    Then use three letters and so on. Using this technique you can make word chains that, if written on joined strips of paper, reach all the way round the classroom. Or make tracks on a wall:

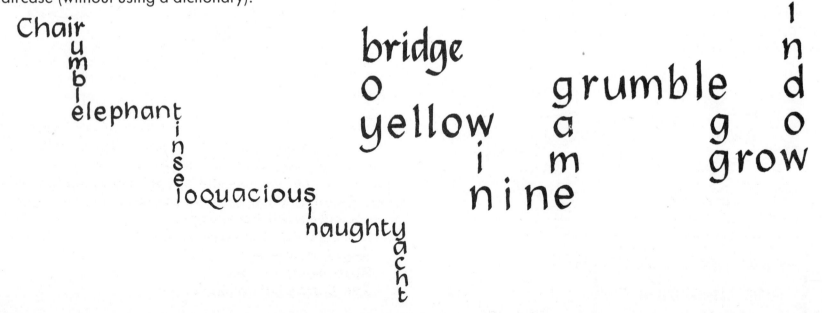

Very able children might be able to design intricate tracks that weave in and out of each other. However, encourage the children to start with short words and simple patterns before moving on to the more complex.

Variation 2

Children who have designed simple word patterns can be introduced to other possibilities for word patterns. For example, stars and stripes:

d r e r i e   today
                   u
rev   a   everyday
          m   s
         c   daily
       r a m   a
         r   yesterday

How many other shapes and patterns can they invent?

Variation 3

Children who can devise interesting and original word patterns can be introduced to acrostics. These are word puzzles written in such a way that the first letters of the words written horizontally spell a word if read vertically. Acrostics can be made so complex that a word can be recognised in each line. For example:

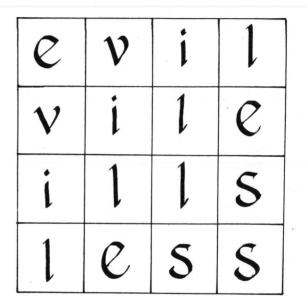

If you want to see whether the children can produce this kind of acrostic it is best to start with four letters and to provide an empty grid for them to work in.

It is much easier, but still thought provoking to write a series of lines based on a forename. Often these turn out to have poetic form. For example:

Gangster I'd like to be
Angry and mean
Razor-sharp and rude
Yes, that's what I'd like for me.

15

Letter scramble

Age range
Five to eleven.

Group size
Individuals.

What you need
Pencil and paper.

What to do
The practice of taking a long word and finding how many shorter words can be made using its letters will be one well-known to most teachers. It can work as a competition if you wish: how many new words can you make using the letters in Rhinoceros or Antarctic.

The game is more difficult if words are chosen that have a limited number of vowels. A good way to 'score' the game is to ask children to check their lists against each other in order to discover who has words that no-one else has thought of. Another way to score is to give double points to words over a certain length eg over four or five letters.

Rhinoceros
nose
rose
on
hose
sore
shine

Antarctic
can
train
tar
tin
attic
arc

Target

Age range
Seven to eleven.

Group size
Individuals.

What you need
Pencil and paper.

What to do
Target involves writing a nine-letter word in the form of a square. For example, dislocate would be written:

DIS
LOC
ATE

The children then have to make as many words as they can, using the letters given, and always including the middle, or target letter, in this case 'O'. Dislocate for instance gives isolate, cold, colt, solid etc.

The missing letters

Age range
Nine to eleven.

Group size
Individuals.

What you need
Pencil and paper.

What to do
This is a game which involves some careful teacher preparation and is based on the kind of exercise that often occurs in IQ tests. For example:

What word goes in the middle to make words into longer words?

ten ( ) elope

Answer: ant

Which four letters start the first word and end the second?

1 ion   2 treat

Answer : ment

There are a variety of formats for these questions. Whole words can occur outside the brackets with a group of letters being the answer. For example:

host ( )bow. Answer: el
man( )man. Answer: ger
mad ( )bush. Answer: am

Or letter groups can occur either side of the bracket with a whole word as the answer. For example:

ar ( )dy . Answer: row.
po ( )nce. Answer: lice.
butc( )mit. Answer: her.

Or the game can be played with compound words or hyphenated words. For example:

lamp( )man. Answer: post.
hand( )link. Answer: cuff.
side ( )stick. Answer: drum.

This last format is probably the easiest to start with.

Word machines

Age range
Five to eleven.

Group size
Individuals.

What you need
Photocopiable pages 107 and 108, pencil and paper.

What to do
Word machines can be used to help children develop a working knowledge of possible letter combinations. After using the machines given, encourage the children to design their own machines, making the rules as inventive and complex as they wish.

Many teachers will be familiar with attribute games played with Logic blocks. In attribute activities a machine is fed with a certain material, performs an operation, and produces a different result. In these games children feed in words instead of mathematical items. Since the variables are so numerous it is recommended that you restrict the material to three or four letter words. In many cases the following ideas use the same track layouts as those provided by ESA for use with Logic blocks. The machines can be as simple or as complex as you wish. Templates for the machines can be found on photocopiable pages 107 and 108.

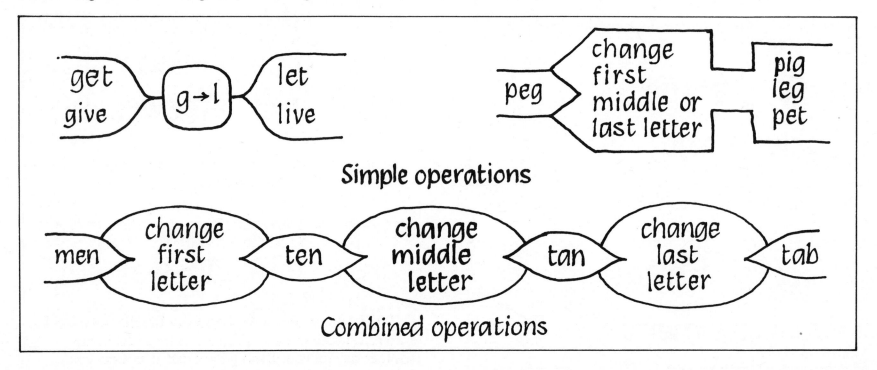

Operations can be more or less specific, but since some operations will result in combinations of letters that will not make known words, it is a good idea to have a reject pile somewhere in the design of the machine. For example:

A word may be held up at any point because the operation is just not possible. These words will be rejected at the appropriate stage. Some discussion about the rejected letter combinations may lead to the discovery of a pattern.

Once children have mastered simple and combined operations children can progress to more complex machines using two or more instructions:

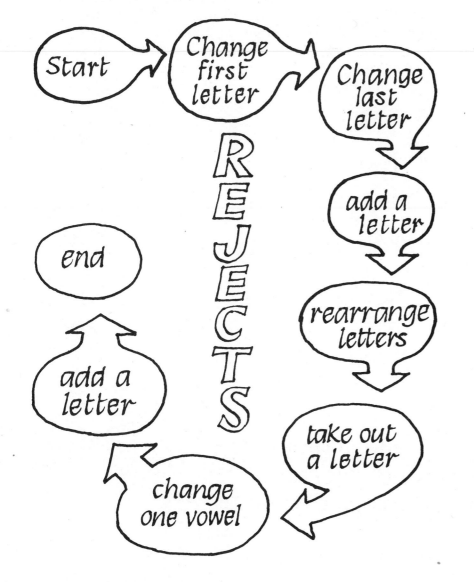

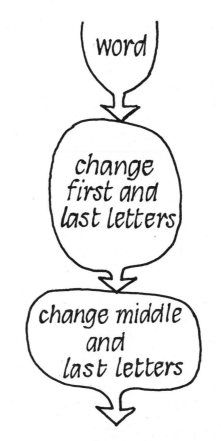

Other operations might be to double the vowel either eg o to ou as in shot to shout, or o to oo as in hot to hoot, or to rearrange the letters and add one.

Word matrices

Age range
Five to eleven.

Group size
Individuals.

What you need
Photocopiable pages 109 to 113, pencil and paper.

What to do
More complex than word machines, matrices can be made so that children have to complete a sequence of operations.

Provide children with a starting word and ask them to fill in the discs. For example, starting with 'bat' arrange the circle according to the arrow instructions.

With practice children may be able to complete a circle. For example starting with 'fun' arrange the words according to the arrow instructions.

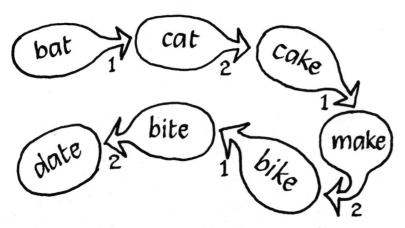

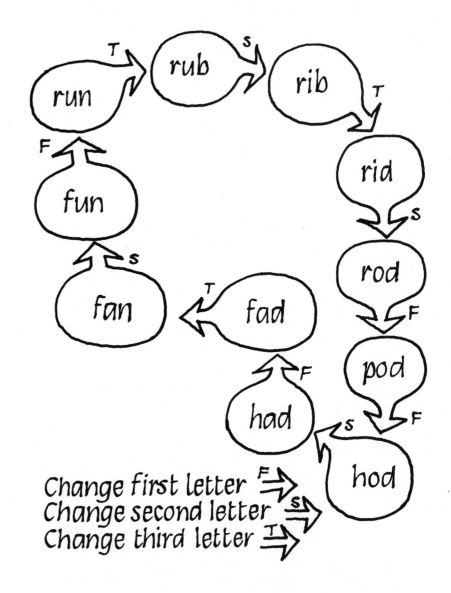

The words given here are only suggestions and you may feel it more useful for children to start with a random word of their own choice and complete the circle. Once started children will very quickly begin to devise their own games using their own words. Confident children will enjoy working with increasingly complex matrices, such as these:

You may wish to provide children with the words in these examples and ask them to use them to fill in the empty matrix. Copies of empty matrices can be found on photocopiable pages 109 to 113. Using given words will demonstrate to the child that a matrix can be completed, but it would be more challenging to give one starting word and let the players work out the other necessary words from there. Children can then go on to use longer words, more difficult layouts and varied operations. The more complex the layout, the more possibilities there are for improvisation.

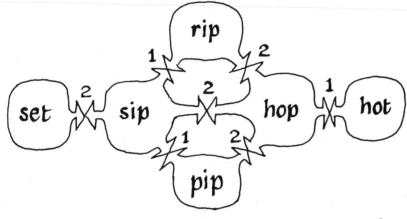

1 letter change ⇒¹ 2 letter change ²⇒

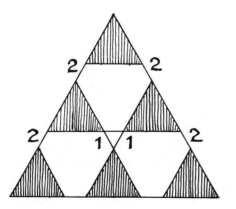

1 letter change 1. 2 letter change 2.

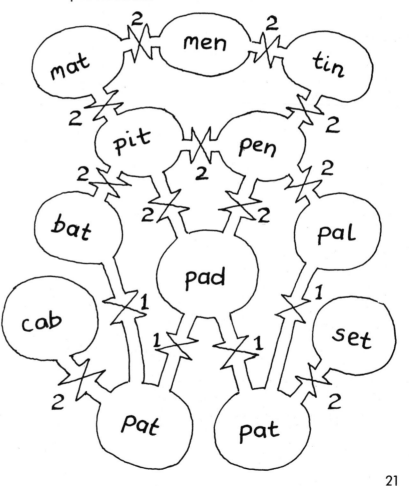

Metamorphosis

Age range
Seven to eleven.

Group size
Individuals.

What you need
Dictionaries, pencil and paper.

What to do
Explain that metamorphosis is the name given to the change which some creatures undergo in the course of growth, such as a caterpillar to a butterfly, or a tadpole to a frog. Can you change one word into an entirely different one by altering one letter at a time.

Problem: Can you turn coal into gold?
Solution: Coal, goal, goad, gold.

Problem: Can you make a fish bite?
Solution: Fish, wish, wise, wide, bide, bite.

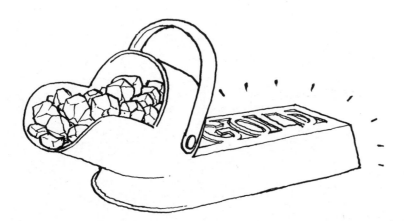

Other problems:
Can you put cash in the bank?
Can you put a foot into a shoe?
Can you turn hate into love?

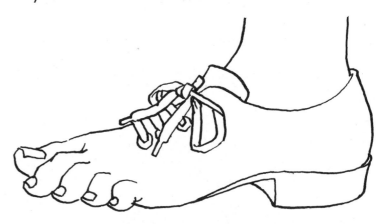

Now ask the children to invent other examples that work well. Explain that it is best to stay with three or four letter words otherwise the game becomes extremely difficult. Obviously both words in the initial problem have to have the same number of letters.

A dictionary may have to be used to check the validity of some words in the solution!

Switch-a-letter

Age range
Eight to eleven.

Group size
Small groups or pairs.

What you need
Pencil and paper.

What to do
In this game the first player says any word which comes to mind. Words with four letters are best and a partner, or other players in the group, take their turns to change one letter at a time, never allowing the same word to be repeated.

Played collaboratively ask each pair or group to see how long they can make their list.

Played competitively ask each pair or group to keep going until one player cannot make a word by changing a single letter and they are then 'out'. For example:

Player 1: PAST
Player 2: PART
Player 3: PORT
Player 4: POST
Player 5: POSE
Player 6: POLE
Player 7: HOLE
Player 8: HOPE etc.

Packs of letters

Age range
Five to eleven.

Group size
Pairs or groups.

What you need
Thin card of different colours to make packs of letters, felt-tipped pens, stop-watch (optional), dictionaries (optional).

What to do
A large number of games can be played using simple home-made packs of cards with letters or words on. It can take quite a while to complete a game with packs of 26 letters however and so initially it is best to start playing with half packs.

Game 1
With young children play 'Pairs'. Make two different coloured packs of cards, each pack containing the 26 letters of the alphabet. Ask the children to lay both packs out randomly on the table, face down. Then they take it in turns to turn up two cards at a time (one from each pack). Any player who turns up two cards having the same letter on can claim the pair. Later ask the children to name the letter by its sound before they can claim the pair.

Game 2
Play 'Pairs' using one pack of capital letters and one pack of lower case letters. To complete a go the child has to turn over an upper and lower case card of the same letter.

Game 3
Have two packs of digraphs eg: th, sh, oo, ch and play 'Pairs' by matching these up.

Game 4

Use packs of words that are frequently used but which are sometimes difficult to spell because they are 'pictureless' and are often confusingly similar eg: which, was, who, there, why, when, went.

Game 5

Using the packs of alphabet cards, let one player shuffle the pack and the other player sort them into alphabetical order as quickly as possible. Players could time each other with a stop-watch. Encourage the use of a dictionary to verify 'answers'.

Game 6

Take a random selection of about six letters and ask the children to sort them alphabetically.

Game 7

Let the children try quick test games on each other eg one player holds up any letter and his partner must quickly find the letters that occur either side of it in the alphabet.

Game 8

Ask pairs of children to use the cards to make words where the letters occur in alphabetical order eg art, deft, fox, bell, chilly, elm.

Game 9

The commercially-produced Lexicon and Kan-U-Go are useful games for the more able children to extend their vocabulary, but it is not difficult to devise other games based on packs of letter cards. Older children may enjoy making an investigation of letter frequency using a page from a book or newspaper, and then making their own game cards with letter values, and rules to the game according to their findings.

The use of letter frequency in English general fiction has been calculated to be:

E T A O H N I S R D L U W M C G F Y P B K V J X Z Q.

So a pack might contain eg:

4 each of E T A O H
4 each of N I S R D L
3 each of U W M C
2 each of G F Y P B
1 of K V J X Z Q.
making a pack of 72 cards.

The variety of games that can be played with letter cards is increased if cards that contain two or more letters are used. Looking in a dictionary will help you discover which are the common double letter combinations, remembering that these combinations occur in the middle and at the end as well as at the beginning of words. Games can be made more or less difficult by altering the make-up of the pack.

Game 10

Share the cards out between the players. Each player turns a card over in turn and leaves it face up in front of him. Any player who sees how to make a word (three letters minimum) from the cards face up on the table can take those letters and place them as a word in front of him. They remain his unless someone else can add a letter or letters to make it into another word. A letter or letters can be added at the beginning, middle or end of the word. Further words continue to be made as cards are turned over and players see the possibilities, until each player has exhausted his original pack. The winner is the player who has the most upturned letters in front of him displayed in words. Letters not placed in words count against a player and must be taken 'card for card' off his final score.

Game 11

Deal each player seven cards which she can look at but must not show to the other players. The players must try to get rid of the cards in their hands either by making a word and laying it in front of them or by adding to a word already on the table. Players can, if they so wish, swap one of their letters with a letter already on the table if that leaves the word on the table intact, (eg a player could change a 'b' in his hand for an 's' on the table by changing SAD to BAD). If a player 'can't go' then he must pick up another letter from the pack that remains in the centre of the table after the hands have been dealt.

Game 12

Make a collection of words that contain either prefixes or suffixes and split the words so that you have a pack of syllable cards and a pack that contains just prefixes and suffixes eg if the prefix/suffix pack contains 'less', that would combine with 'home' or 'child' or 'friend' or 'care' in the syllable pack.

List of common prefixes

ab– (away from) as in absent, abstain
ad– (towards, against) as in advance, adverse
aero– (air) as in aeroplane
ante– (before) as in ante-natal
anti– (against) as in antipathy
auto– (self) as in automatic, autobiography
bi– (two) as in bicycle, bi-centenary
con– (together) as in contract, conversation
contra– (against) as in contradiction
de– (down from, out of) as in deflate, descent
ex– (out of) as in exhaust, exit, extract

extra– (outside) as in extraordinary, extradite
in– (in, into or 'not') as in injection, inefficient
inter– (between) as in interchangeable
per– (through) as in permit, pervade
pre– (before) as in prefix, premature
pro– (forwards) as in propel, project
semi– (half) as in semi-detached, semi-circle
sub– (under, less than) as in submarine, subway
super– (over, more than) as in supernatural
tele– (far off) as in telephone, television
trans– (across) as in transmit, transatlantic
tri– (three) as in triangle, trident, tripod
ultra– (beyond) as in ultrasonic, ultraviolet
un– (not) as in unprepared, unfit, unnecessary
dis– (apart, not) as in disinfect, disappear.

List of common suffixes

–or as in director
–ite as in graphite
–dom as in kingdom, freedom
–ty as in plenty, shanty
–ing as in helping
–tion as in station

—age as in mileage
—let as in piglet
—ern as in southern
—ish as in sheepish
—able as in likeable
—est as in fastest
—ist as in chemist, dentist
—ness as in likeness
—hood as in childhood, parenthood
—ship as in friendship
—ment as in payment, complement
—sion as in pension, tension
—ful as in careful, fretful
—ly as in shapely, hardly
—like as in doglike, fishlike
—some as in lonesome
—less as in careless, friendless
—wards as in windwards, homewards.

So if a pack contained these prefixes and suffixes the second pack would need to contain words such as 'help' (to go with -ful, -less, -ing, -er) and 'king' (to go with —ly, and —dom) and 'tract' (to go with pro—, ex—, de—) and 'cycle' (to go with bi— and tri—) etc.

Develop the rules of the game in the same way as rules for other card games. You could, for instance deal all the cards from one pack and leave the other pack in the centre. In turn players pick a card from the centre pack, hoping they can match it with a card in their hand. If this is not possible they leave it upturned in a 'discard' pile next to the centre pack. The next player can then choose to pick up either from the centre pack or the discard pack. The final player to match up all the cards in his hands wins.

With younger children, you could give one group of children a prefix/suffix card and another group syllable cards. One group stands at one side of the room, the

other group at the other. Then at a signal each child has to find a partner. Then each pair is asked to read their joint word, before the cards are swapped around for another go.

Game boards

Age range
Five to eleven.

Group size
Pairs or small groups.

What you need
Cardboard, pencil, ruler, coloured felt-tipped pens, dice, photocopiable pages 114 to 116.

What to do
You may want to combine any of the card games (on pages 24 to 28) with a playing board. For instance, when children match a capital letter and a lower case letter in Game 1 they could move a space or two on a game board. Boards can be easily devised and made interesting by including instructions, either written on the board itself or on a separate pack of chance cards. You could colour every fifth place red and indicate that a player who lands on, say, a red place must pick up a chance card.

Instructions might include:
- move on two places
- miss a turn
- give one card to another player
- pick up two cards from the central pack.

With some games, players would use a die and take their turn on the board before attempting to make words with their letters. The aim of the game would then be to reach the last square *and* to finish all the cards in their hand.

Photocopiable patterns for making these boards can be found on pages 114 to 116. The patterns should be stuck to card and made interesting by the addition of colour and perhaps pictures.

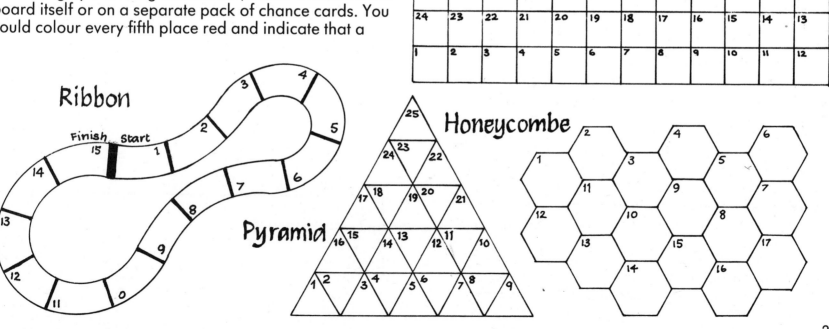

Squares / end

25	26	27	28	29	30	31	32	33	34	35	36
24	23	22	21	20	19	18	17	16	15	14	13
1	2	3	4	5	6	7	8	9	10	11	12

Ribbon

Pyramid

Honeycombe

Word squares

Age range
Nine to eleven.

Group size
Small groups.

What you need
Paper divided into 36 squares, pencils.

What to do
Each player has a square of paper ruled into 36 smaller squares – the size more or less depending on the age of the children. Each player calls out a letter and all the players can, but are not obliged to, write it into their grid in any place that might help them build words both down and across.

There should be a small pause for thinking time between each letter being called. When a player's turn to call a letter arrives, they will of course call one that is of most use to them. After a certain number of turns the teacher should call a halt and players check each other's grids for the number of words they have made.

If the first ten letters are A S T E O L M B R P; the two grids show two possible solutions so far:

Player A has formed two words, 'malt' and 'step' and is looking to finish ra . . . .
Player B has formed two words 'sat' and 'lot' and has three started: bl . . . , me . . . , and sp . . . .

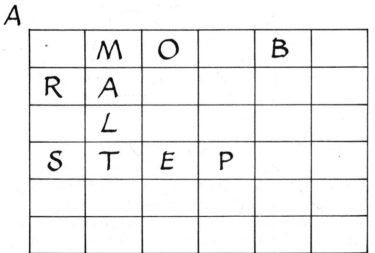

Spoonerisms

Age range
Seven to eleven.

Group size
Whole class.

What you need
Pencil and paper, tape-recorder (optional), stop-watch (optional).

What to do
Spoonerisms occur when you transpose the initial sounds of words, either letters or syllables. They are named after Reverend William Spooner (1844–1930), an Oxford scholar who was a noted perpetrator of this form of word-play.

Game 1
Provide simple sentences and ask children to turn them into spoonerisms. One of the most famous of the Reverend Spooner's mix-ups was:

'Sir, you have deliberately tasted two whole worms'
(Sir, you have deliberately wasted two whole terms').
or
Provide spoonerisms which have to be translated back into sensible sentences. Competition can be introduced by placing a limit on the time allowed to 'solve' the spoonerism.

Game 2
Divide the class into pairs. Suggest a scenario, such as two people meeting for the first time at a party, or a shop assistant and customer, or a waiter and restaurant guest, or a football player and referee, or a TV repairman and a householder.

Now each pair of children has to devise a conversation, taking on the roles defined, but inventing spoonerisms as the conversation progresses.

Each pair could make a record of their invented conversation to read back to the class, or pairs could take it in turns to play their conversation into a tape-recorder.

TV Repairman: Your belevisions definitely token.
Householder: But why can't you wake it merk.
Repairman: I haven't got the pight rart with me. I'll have to go shack to the bop to get it.
Householder: But I want to tatch the welevision show.
Repairman: I'm morry sadam, there's nothing I dan co!

Written spoonerisms do not indicate the amusement as well as spoken versions can.

Cartoon bubbles

Age range
Seven to eleven.

Group size
Pairs.

What you need
Newspapers and comics, scissors, correcting fluid, felt-tipped pens.

What to do
To write speech bubbles into cartoons will require some preparation, but it can be done by the children themselves.

Ask the children to work in pairs to cut out comic strips from newspapers or short cartoon stories from comics. Then get one member of the pair to white out the words inside the speech bubbles for the partner to fill in, using the correcting fluid. Each child can then make up the story, based on the pictures, and read it back to their partner.

Alternatively, you can white out speech bubbles yourself and photocopy the altered cartoon to hand out to a group. All the children in the group can then fill in the bubbles to give meaning to the set of pictures and compare their different versions at the end.

Speed marathon writing

Age range
Seven to eleven.

Group size
Whole class or groups.

What you need
Pencil and paper.

What to do
A speed marathon, sometimes known as a composition derby, is a good way to help children to realise how much they are capable of writing in a short space of time. The idea is that they experience the flow of writing at speed without, on this occasion, any serious concern with content or spelling.

Ask the class, or a group, to sit with only a pencil and copious amounts of paper. Give the following instructions:

- You have five minutes to write as much as you possibly can, as fast as you can.
- I will tell you when each minute goes by.
- You can write whatever you want to, but it must make sense, and you must not simply repeat yourself. If you can't think of anything to write or you get stuck, write 'I can't think of anything to write at the moment. Oh, I know, I will write about my old aunt Jemima . . .' or 'I am stuck at the moment and thinking of what to write. I think I will write about my cat who . . .'.
- Don't worry about spelling, but the writing must be legible enough for someone else to read.
- Begin.

At the end of the time period, which can of course be altered depending on the age of the children, ask each child to swap their writing with the child next to them who adds up the number of words written. The child that has written the most wins. It is a good idea to play the game two or three times over a period of time, in order that children can compete against their previous performance.

Sending messages

This section contains games and activities designed to encourage children to send and receive messages in a variety of ways.

There are many ways of getting a class of children to communicate with each other. Encourage them to start sending memos, or let them write notes using words and letters cut from magazines and newspapers, choosing their own audience and purpose. To give the children an understanding of the need for precise use of language in some messages ask them to write instructions for each other to go with maps or diagrams. Letter writing will give the children some idea of the different conventions that apply to different types of writing. For example, writing addresses means conforming with certain conventions to do with commas, capital letters and layout. Other activities are suggested as one way of giving children rehearsal in spoken language. 'Talking games' challenge children to talk for particular purposes – to explain to the rest of the group what they accept as obvious, or to use precise language in the giving of instructions, or to engage in exploratory talk. In these respects they can be used to build children's confidence with speech.

In a class where messages of all sorts are regularly sent and received, children will begin to see themselves as part of a language community.

Real letters and fantasy letters

Age range
Seven to eleven.

Group size
Whole class.

What you need
Pencil and paper; a variety of reference material such as magazines, newspapers, leaflets, travel brochures etc.

What to do
Letter writing will be more meaningful for children if the letter, instead of being merely an exercise, has a genuine purpose and the possibility of a reply.

There are a huge number of possible destinations for letters for children. Try sending letters to:

- The Queen.
- The Prime Minister.
- The town mayor.
- The local MP.
- Local or national radio or television.
- Magazines and newspapers of all sorts, perhaps to a 'Problem page'.
- Celebrities of all kinds, eg children's authors, sports or TV personalities, poets.
- Local firms, especially travel agents, requesting literature.
- Charities such as Oxfam, Shelter and the RSPCA.
- National bodies and pressure groups like The Sports Council, The Arts Council, The National Trust, The Ramblers' Association, Greenpeace, The Milk Marketing Board etc.

- Other classes, to other teachers, to the headteacher, to other local schools, to schools in other countries, to penfriends.

It is, of course, possible to send letters to imaginary destinations. If the children try this, why not make the sender an imaginary person too? What would a traveller from another planet have to say about the earth when writing home?

Perhaps you could ask the children to pick up some small object in the room and name it eg Mavis White, the stick of chalk; Slim Brown, the paint brush; Violet Vinyl, the pencil case etc. Have series of naming ceremonies or baptisms if you wish! Now these objects can write to each other describing the place they live!

Suzy Scrawl, the crayon, for example, waxes lyrical to Peter Page. She proclaims her undying love for him and tells him of the misery of her life behind the waste paper basket in the secretary's office.

What a location for a vacation

Age range
Nine to eleven.

Group size
Whole class.

What you need
Holiday brochures, map of Europe, pencil and paper.

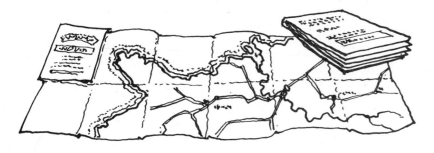

What to do
Holiday brochures are often a source of interest to children. Point out that the intention of such brochures is to show each location in the best possible light then get the class to invent a holiday pamphlet for the place where a classroom object lives. Explain that the pamphlet needs to persuade other objects to come for a holiday in the various locations and therefore has to expound the delights to be had when visiting eg Suzy Scrawl's waste paper basket, or perhaps the broom cupboard, or the far corner of the playground. You will, of course, need to encourage children to browse through various genuine brochures to get a feel for the type of language used.

Activity 2
Another 'message activity' that can arise out of the study of holiday brochures is a 'You have won a prize' letter. Ask the class to assume that a friend has won a holiday as a prize in a competition. They have to make up a smart package describing the holiday to send to him. They should include such details as prices, maps, suggested sightseeing trips, references from others who have been on a similar holiday etc.

Activity 3
They could invent the very worst kind of holiday that a friend would wish to go on, eg 'Dear Miss Vertigo, We are very pleased to inform you that you have just won a fabulous hang-gliding holiday in our "What a location for a vacation" competition . . . and the wonderful climax of your holiday will come when you have the chance to dive off the top of the Eiger, Europe's most dangerous mountain, notorious for the number of lives it has claimed'.

Activity 4
Give the children holiday brochures and a road map of Europe and ask them to plan a route to the destination of their choice and then pass it over to a friend to find their way through the map to the resort.

Headlines!

Age range
Nine to eleven.

Group size
Small groups.

What you need
Newspapers, scissors, pencil and paper.

What to do
Headlines are simple bold messages. Newspapers very often have strange headlines.

Activity 1
Get the groups of children to hunt through some old newspapers. How many odd, unusual or interesting headlines can they find out and collect? Then ask the class to write short stories explaining what one or two of the headlines might mean.

Activity 2
Get the children to pretend they are newspaper editors and have to write the headlines.

Cut out some newspaper stories yourself without a headline and give them to a group of children. Ask them to write a headline and see if it matches the original. Later they can cut out their own stories from newspapers and hand them on to friends to write headlines.

Activity 3
After discussing the kind of language used and the format of real headlines play a 'Good News, Bad News' game asking the children to invent contrasting headlines

for the same event. For example:

'Vicar Sees The Light' – 'Hole Found in Church Roof'.

Alternatively give the children the first half of a pair of headlines and ask them to provide the second.

For example:

'Judo to be Taught in Schools' . . .

'Traffic Jam Causes Chaos' . . .

Another variation is to invent a 'misleading' headline and then write a short paragraph underneath to explain it. For example:

'Man Marries His Daughter' – A vicar, Reverend Robert Church, conducted the wedding ceremony of his daughter Valerie Church, yesterday . . . .

Picture messages

Age range
Five to eleven.

Group size
Whole class.

What you need
Magazine pictures and photographs.

What to do
This game teaches children to think carefully about the 'message' that can be received from a picture.

Place a large picture or photograph where all the children can see it. Then you make statements, related to the photograph to which the children's response can only be 'true', 'false' or 'can't tell'. For instance, a picture of a lorry driver and his mate in their cab would require such statements as:

A man is driving a car.
He is holding the steering wheel.
He has had egg and bacon for breakfast.
The men are brothers.
The lorry is moving.
The men's names are Fred and Frank.
The driver has blond hair.

Secret languages

Age range
Seven to eleven.

Group size
Pairs.

What you need
Books; photocopiable page 117; pencil and paper; commercial 'magic' pens, lemon juice or milk.

What to do
Present the children with a few examples of the way codes can be invented, and then ask them to send messages in code to each other, inventing their own if they are able. There are numerous letter codes. The following are simple examples:

You can make one by leaving gaps in the wrong place.
CANY OUM AKE UPA SECR ETC ODE?
You can make one by writing words backwards.
NAC OUY EKAM PU A TERCES EDOC?
You can make one by inserting the less common letters at random intervals.
CAQN YOQU MAXKE UZP AX SEY CRETQ COZ DE?
You can make one by swapping each letter with its neighbour, first with second, third with fourth etc, and then joining all the words together.
ACYNUOAMEKPUSACEERCTDOE?

Another way of inventing a code involves using a book. The encoder writes three numbers to identify one word:
● The page number
● The line number
● The word number on that line.

So the coded message is a list of three connected numbers. The decoder uses the same book to turn the numbers back into words.

An old telephone can be used as a device for inventing a code, or the dial can be made using card. Photocopiable page 117 has a pattern for this which can be cut out and stuck on card.

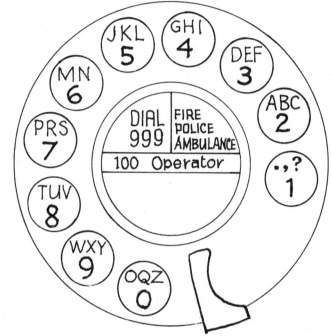

Since each number might represent any of up to three letters, deciphering a telephone code is not easy!

It is not difficult to spend a great deal of time studying codes, perhaps including work on the history of the alphabet from cave painting through hieroglyphics, and the Phoenician, Greek and Roman alphabets to the present day versions. There are in fact 65 alphabets in use in the world. One of the shortest is used in Hawaii – AEHIKLMNOPUW. How many words can children make using this alphabet? What might they use in place of words that they cannot make? You could also look at established codes like Morse, semaphore, sign language for the deaf, shorthand, and number codes like postcodes and telephone numbers. Some children might be interested in studying the various non-verbal ways of signalling that have been devised over the years such as railway signals, the cricket umpire's signs to the scorer, the signals used by a policeman on traffic duty, the Navy's special flag signals etc. Indeed exploration of these topics could turn into a quite sophisticated study of symbolism.

Activity 2
Cryptic and entertaining messages can be sent using visual clues. For example:

OURRU

(I think I am going to be a footballer. Oh you are, are you!)

Extend this technique into story writing, or perhaps it should be called story composing. Remember that children will enjoy trying to decipher messages as much as they will composing them.

Activity 3
Messages sent in code can be made interesting to decipher if written in invisible ink. There are pens on the market that write in invisible ink which becomes visible if scribbled over with a second 'magic' pen, but making your own invisible ink is also possible. Messages written in lemon juice or milk will become invisible as they dry. To make the message reappear heat the paper over a radiator or in an oven on a very low heat. You can also write an invisible message by pressing hard on two sheets of paper, the top one dry but the bottom one wet. The wet sheet will reveal the message when held to the light but the indentation will disappear as it dries. To reveal the message simply dampen the paper once more.

Treasure hunt

Age range
Seven to eleven.

Group size
Pairs or small groups.

What you need
Small object to hide, pencil and paper, PE equipment, blindfold (optional).

What to do
Ask a child to place a small object like a coin somewhere in the school and then to write precise instructions describing the route to be followed to find the object (obviously the exact location must not be named in the instructions). Get another child to follow the instructions to find the object and then report back on the accuracy of the instructions.

Game 2
Ask the pairs or groups of children to draw a desert island on a large piece of paper including the names of various locations. Having decided where they are going to bury the treasure and noted down the place on a separate slip of paper, ask them to write a set of instructions, on a sheet of paper made to look like an authentic piece of parchment, giving a route for someone else to follow. For older children a scale could be included on the map eg 1 cm = 1 km so that the instructions might, for instance, read: 'Land at Shark's Bay and walk 5 km north to the Mangrove Swamp. Head west for 7 km crossing the river at Shallow Point and then turning south etc'. When the treasure hunters

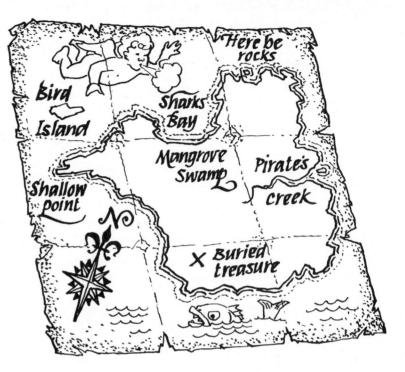

are sure they have found the correct spot to start digging they declare it to the map drawers who have to reveal the location of the treasure on their slips of paper.

Game 3
In a hall, when the PE equipment is arranged for use, get a child to stand blindfolded at one end. A partner has to guide the blindfolded child by giving careful instructions in order to help them move to the opposite end of the hall without touching anything. With younger children it is a good idea to give the blindfolded child a silent guide, who does not direct but ensures that nobody actually bumps into or trips over equipment!

Telephone messages

Age range
Five to eleven.

Group size
Individuals or pairs.

What you need
Toy telephone; optional: Lego bricks, screen, various objects.

What to do
A telephone is a useful way of helping children to invent conversations less self-consciously than if they have to talk face to face. The telephone can also be used to play a game where one child conducts a conversation from her end (giving no very obvious clues) with an imaginary famous person on the other end of the line. The partner, or the rest of the class must listen carefully to find out 'who's there'.

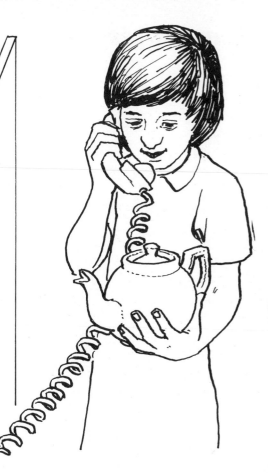

Variation
To practise description with younger children place a screen between two children who have a telephone each.

One child holds an object where the partner cannot see it and then describes what it looks like so that the partner can guess. A variation of this is to ask the first child to build a structure from Lego, or building bricks. The second child has to build an identical structure to the original following detailed instructions given to him by the original builder. Play the same game with simple outline drawings of objects.

Chinese whispers

Age range
Five to eleven.

Group size
Whole class.

What you need
No specific requirements.

What to do
Chinese whispers is one way of helping children to realise the importance of clear speech when sending a verbal message and of careful listening when receiving one. Ask the class to sit in a circle, hand one child a written message and ask her to whisper it into the ear of her neighbour without anyone else hearing. As the message gets passed around the circle it will inevitably change, especially if the original message had a tongue-twisting element such as send me a copper-bottomed coffee pot. The final version of the message is likely to give rise to much hilarity and hopefully a realisation of the need for clarity of diction.

Game 2
Another game that can be played with the class sitting in a circle is 'letter connections'. Each participant has to give a word that starts with the last letter of the previous word. So if the first child says 'top', the second perhaps might say 'palm' and the third 'megalomania' etc.

Game 3
'Word connection' is a version of 'Letter connection' which simply demands that one word must have some connection with the previous one to count as a valid follow-on eg hand, foot, ball, round, penny, etc. Needless to say, this version requires a wise, and firm, umpire.

Deduction

Age range
Five to eleven.

Group size
Whole class.

What you need
Teacher preparation.

What to do
'Deduction' asks the children to put together information from two, separate messages to acquire the answer to a question. As the name implies it is a game intended to encourage careful thinking. You will have to devise a pair of sentences and a complementary question for the children. It should be possible to find the answer to the question only by taking into account the facts given in both sentences and then making a deduction. Here are some examples:

- Father has a spade in his hand and he is going into the garden.
  He takes his coat off.
  What is the weather like?

- I am watching some birds.
  The keeper is feeding them from a bucket of fish.
  Where am I?

- My hands are on the wheel. My foot is on the brake.
  What am I doing?

- A man is lying back in a chair. Another man is bending over him holding a mirror.
  What is happening?

- The lady is in the market. She is calling out 'All fresh today. Lovely colours. Buy a bunch now'.
  What is she selling?

- Two boys are going swimming. Mother says 'You will look after John, won't you, David?'
  Which boy is the best swimmer?

- She buys her ticket. She walks on to the platform and waits.
  Where is she?

Interesting discussions can arise when deciding which answers are valid and which are not.

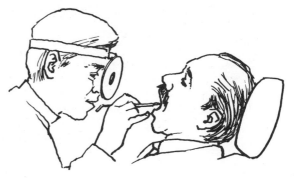

Misleading messages

Age range
Five to eleven.

Group size
Whole class.

What you need
Teacher preparation.

What to do
This is a variation on 'Deduction' (see page 45). Again it requires teacher preparation. The simplest version requires that a sentence be read out to children which contains an obvious incongruity for them to spot.

For example: The blind man identified the bank robbers from police photographs.

A more taxing way to play is to increase the listening time for participants and allow the incongruous element to be obvious only when the listener connects sentences at a distance from one another in the passage.

For example: I got up very early the next morning. The sun was already beating down on the parched brown grass fields around my camp. Despite the fact that I had only a stick to protect me I was looking forward to another day hunting the wolf which had been killing the sheep in this area. We left camp immediately after breakfast and it was not long before we came across the wolf, resting by a rock. The huge creature turned to face us, his eyes glowing bright in the moonlight. Suddenly he started to run towards us. I raised my stick in front of my face as he leapt at me . . . .

Game 2

Odd man out is very simple and best for young players. You simply call out a list of items for the class to identify the 'odd one out' from the list eg 'car, lorry, van, bus, bicycle, tractor'. The bicycle is the odd one out since all the others have more than two wheels. It is instructive to discuss with children the reasons why a certain item is the odd one out, and in many instances you will discover that they will find a different reason for the answer than the one you had in mind. For instance, in the example given it could be that the bicycle is the only one without an engine. The children may even come up with a different answer to the one intended and be able to justify it to everyone's satisfaction.

Game 3

Cloze, normally a reading exercise, can be played as a listening game. The teacher needs to prepare a story or passage with certain words missed out. Words are deleted either because they come at regular intervals or because they have something in common, eg in a story about a zoo it might be possible to delete the names of all the animals if the passage gives a clue to their identity. The class then has to suggest possible insertions at those places where you have left a blank. Before the passage is read out of course, you must explain that they should listen carefully for contextual clues in order to supply the missing words. It makes reading easier if the missing words are substituted by some nonsense word or sound, perhaps one invented by the children. Experienced players could prepare passages to read to their friends or a small group, or even write their own story with missing words for others to guess.

Who's she?

Age range
Seven to eleven.

Group size
Individuals or groups.

What you need
Pencil and paper.

What to do
What kind of messages do children hear constantly repeated to them. Ask who gets nagged. Who nags? Mother, father, friends, teacher? Do the children find themselves saying the same thing over and over again to somebody?

Ask the children, individually or in groups, to make as long a list as they can and then arrange them in some kind of order, eg Mums' sayings, brothers' sayings, teachers' sayings. Perhaps these could be read out with readers trying to get the exact tone of voice of the original 'nagger'. Or perhaps write the sayings on slips of paper and collect them in a class book.

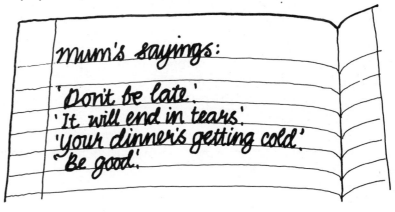

Questions and answers

Age range
Nine to eleven.

Group size
Individuals;
Whole class (Game 2).

What you need
Pencil and paper.

What to do
Get each child to write down five questions of any kind, after explaining to them that these questions should be as imaginative and inventive as possible. You could stipulate that the questions have to be on a certain theme eg animals:

How was the whale built?

Why do cats like dustbins?

What happens in a zoo when the people go home?

Then ask the children to swap their questions and answer the questions they have been given. The results can be read out round the class and the best might be collected together in a book or on a wall display.

Game 2
'Yes, No, I don't know' is another questions and answers game, for a large group or the whole class.

One child sits in the hot seat and others sitting in a semi-circle around fire a variety of questions at her.

The 'hot seat' child must answer the questions without answering 'Yes', 'No' or 'I don't know'. The child whose question makes the answerer slip up is the next in the 'hot seat'. Played well, the game is a battle of wits with

one side having to think of ingenious questions and the other having to be resourceful to avoid the taboo words. If the 'hot seat' child becomes too clever at doing this then other forbidden words can be added to the list, like 'black', 'white', all numbers, days, months etc.

Story chains

Age range
Five to eleven.

Group size
Whole class.

What you need
Teacher story; pictures (variation 2); a variety of different objects (variation 3).

What to do
With the class sitting in a circle start to tell them a story. Each child then adds his own short contribution to carry the story forward. Even the most shy child can usually make a contribution if it is made clear that even a very short addition to the story is valued.

Variation 1
Specify that each child in the circle must only add one sentence.

Variation 2
For younger children provide a sequence of large pictures for them to talk about, or ask them to guess how the story might continue in the next picture by holding up the first one.

Variation 3
Have an object (shoe, plastic brick or whatever) that is thrown from child to child in the circle. Whoever receives it must continue the story for a short while before throwing the object to another child and passing the story on.

Variation 4
For older children have two teams facing one another. The first child on one team starts a story, and then the first child on the opposite team has to try to subvert that story by continuing with a statement that starts 'but . . . '. Continue until the story returns to the second child in team 1 who has to try to re-establish the story, and so on.

Scenario games

Age range
Nine to eleven.

Group size
Whole class divided into groups.

What you need
Pencil and paper, an assortment of household items, a lady's handbag containing a variety of items.

What to do
Split the class into groups and explain that you are going to give each group a different 'situation' to discuss and write about. They then have to report back to the rest of the class about what they have been doing.

Game 1
Choose one of the following situations:
- Explain that you are all criminals in a high security prison but that an escape route has been discovered. There will only be time for one individual to use it though. Each member of the group must argue why he should be the one to escape.
- You are all circus folk deciding which act should 'top the bill'.
- You are all animals in a zoo planning the escape (of one).
- You are toys in a cupboard. Which is the most loved by the owner?

Each group must report back to the class at the end of the game session.

Game 2
Explain that you are living in the year 2600. There has been a nuclear war and you have all recently emerged from the shelters. Have a number of bags with household items in them of various sorts eg corkscrew, whisk, washing-up liquid bottle, toothbrush, plug etc. Ask the group to discuss what they can deduce about the people of the twentieth century by looking at these objects which have suddenly been revealed at the bottom of craters, trying to imagine what they could possibly have been used for. At the end of the session get the group to explain their conclusions to the rest of the class.

An alternative scenario could be the finding of the twentieth century objects by a tribe who have been cut off from civilisation, perhaps because of the density of the forest in which they live, or because they live on a remote desert island.

Other problems could later be given to the detective teams:

- Interview a gang of three criminals (who have been primed by you) to discover who actually shot a security van driver.
- Interview witnesses to an accident (witnesses can again be children who have had time to prepare their stories) to discover who is to blame.
- Interrogate two boys who have been fighting and attempt to construct a coherent account of the events that led to the violence (the interviewees must be given time to get their story together).

Game 3

Explain to the group that they are a team of detectives. Present them with a handbag that contains a variety of items likely to be found in a lady's handbag, eg a shopping list, an empty purse, a photograph, a book, a key, make-up, nail scissors etc but include nothing that might be a clue to a specific identity. Now tell the detectives that the handbag was found on an unidentified body that has recently been dragged from a local river. Ask the teams to try to build up a picture of the woman's personality and background based on the evidence before them, and perhaps provide some ideas as to how and why she died. Again, after a while get the groups to compare their portraits.

Games with sentences and parts of speech

Games can be used to give children an intuitive feel for the structure of language.

Play with language also provides the opportunity to make children aware of their unconscious knowledge about language. The structure of English may be complex but the teacher who carefully increases a child's knowledge of the underlying structure of language is helping to increase that child's feeling of power over language. Many young children take pride in acquiring technical jargon. Most children are familiar with using specialised language in mathematics, and there seems no good reason why they should not know that words in sentences have special labels and particular functions. Of course, language is not a collection of sentences. Indeed talk is normally done in chunks of meaning below the organisational level of the sentence. Perhaps this is why, as most teachers would concede, a great many children have difficulty planning sentences in their writing. These children obviously need help in understanding what a sentence is, ie a number of words that carry a complete meaning and a certain grammatical structure. They also have to be aware that it is important to make one's meaning explicit to an audience. But to try to teach sentence construction as part of a commentary on a child's general writing is fraught with difficulties, not the least of which is the danger that you encourage the child to concentrate less on the content of his writing and more on the structure. Children who are asked to work with sentences separated out from a narrative, as the games in this section demand, may more easily learn to recognise the form and so transfer that learning back into their narrative writing, perhaps at the redrafting stage.

Sentence search

Age range
Five to eleven.

Group size
Individuals, pairs or groups.

What you need
Pencil and paper; stop-watches; alphabet cards (Game 3); blackboard and chalk (Game 4).

What to do
These games require the children to devise sentences that meet a particular set of specifications. The games can be played with individuals, pairs or groups of children competing against the clock, to find the most sentences, or simply for the sake of interest and experiment.

Game 1
Make a search for sentences that use only words beginning with the same letter. For example:
An ancient Armenian angered an armadillo.

This game can be used to introduce alliteration, pointing out that the technique is not likely to be successful if used in this excessive form in a poem!

Game 2
Write any sentence. Now use the initial letters of all the words in that sentence as the initial letters of all the words in other sentences. For example: taking the sentence 'Daddy wouldn't buy me a Bow-wow', make up as many sentences as you can in which the words start with the letters D, W, B, M, A and B, no matter how

ridiculous. For example: David wandered behind my apricot bush.

Alternatively, write out the name of a town, or country and make up a message using words which begin with the letters that spell that name, eg LEEDS – Let's eat each dish slowly.

Game 1

An ancient Armenian angered an armadillo.
We wish to wear warm woolies.
Slippery snakes slide silently.

Game 2

Leeds: Let's eat each dish slowly.
Bristol: Boys run in style towards open lanes.

Game 3

This game requires a set of alphabet cards (see pages 24 to 28 for card games).

Place the pack face down in the centre of the table. The first player turns over a card and says a word beginning with the letter that is turned up. The next player turns up a letter and says a word that starts with that letter but which also follows the first word and helps to build a sentence. Each player adds a word to the sentence in turn. At any point a player can shout 'full stop', if he thinks a sentence is complete. Players are allowed to pass, but should be encouraged to use their ingenuity to find a word each time.

Game 4

Groups of children can combine to write sentences. One way is to divide the children into groups of say six. The first child has to write the first word of a sentence on a piece of paper and pass it on for the second team member to add the second word. Each member adds a word bearing in mind that the last child must add the final word of the sentence. To complete a sentence successfully in this manner is not easy and children who can play the game successfully will be well on the way to an understanding of sentence construction.

If you wish to play the game with the whole class then each group member could write his contribution to the sentence on the blackboard rather than on paper so that everyone can see. The first player in each group runs to the blackboard and writes a word, then runs back to the group and hands the chalk to the second player who does likewise, and so on. They are allowed to add words either in front of, or after, what is already on the board. For older children increase the challenge by requiring each team member to make two or even three contributions before the sentence can end.

Game 5

Write sentences where most of the words contain the same sound. For example: Bert dirtied thirty shirts.

These sentences often turn out to be 'tongue-twisters' and the children will enjoy reading their 'tongue-twisters' to each other at speed.

Game 6

Write a story of seven sentences. Each sentence must have just seven words. Try the same exercise with different numbers.

Telegrams

Age range
Nine to eleven.

Group size
Whole class.

What you need
Pencil and paper.

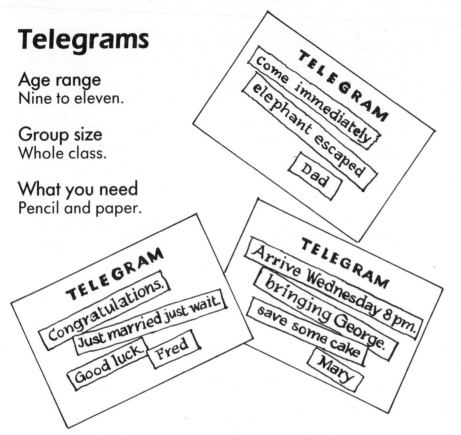

What to do
Make up telegrams to show the children which words form the core of a sentence and which can be omitted without meaning being lost, eg definite and indefinite articles.

Ask the class to compare messages of any 50 words and then experiment to see how many words can be removed without sacrificing the meaning. Each child can test his work by asking a friend to read his telegram and reconstruct its meaning as it would be expressed in normal speech. How closely does the reconstruction match the original message?

Game 2
Write a very long sentence such as the following:

I was sitting on top of my horse one day at the top of a set of swimming pool diving boards when it slipped on a banana skin and we both tumbled into the water, which was not as warm as I would have wished it.

Now challenge the children to reduce the sentence in stages, at each turn substituting just one word for two that occur in the sentence. For example:
    Move one: change 'banana skin' to 'cherry'.
    Move two: change 'both tumbled' to 'fell'.
    Move three: 'diving boards' is dropped and 'steps' substituted and so on until the sentence becomes irreducible.

Game 3
Write a very short sentence and get the children to make it longer by changing one of the words in it for two different words. For example:
    I had a little nut tree.
    Move one: I had a great big nut tree.
    Move two: Miss Muffet had a great big nut tree.
    Move three: Miss Muffet climbed up a great big nut tree.
And so on.

Classified ads

Age range
Nine to eleven.

Group size
Small groups.

What you need
Newspapers, pencil and paper.

What to do
Classified advertisements in local and national newspapers reduce sentences to bare minimums (which are rarely full sentences) in order to save space. Provide the children with the 'Classified ads' pages from local newspapers and explore the various abbreviations used. For example:

MOT in car advertisements
and FGCH in house advertisements
and £50 ONO.

Ask the children to rewrite the adverts in full sentences. So:

Small S/C flat, FGCH, all Mod cons, £200 pcm
Tel: 68954

would become:

A small self-contained flat is available for rent. It has full gas central heating and all modern conveniences. It costs £200 per calendar month. Please telephone 68954 for further information.

Mobius sentences

Age range
Nine to eleven.

Group size
Individuals.

What you need
Paper, scissors, pencils.

What to do
A Mobius sentence is an amusing device. It is a strip with only one side. Cut a piece of paper about 1 cm wide and 50 cm long and then join it with just one twist.

If you put your pencil on it and draw a line you should be able to go round and round both sides without taking the pencil off. Some sentences can go round and round in this manner. Ask the children if they can invent one and then write it on a Mobius strip. For example:

When you get out of a taxi, the driver must smile and wait for a tip because he knows that when you get out of a taxi . . . .

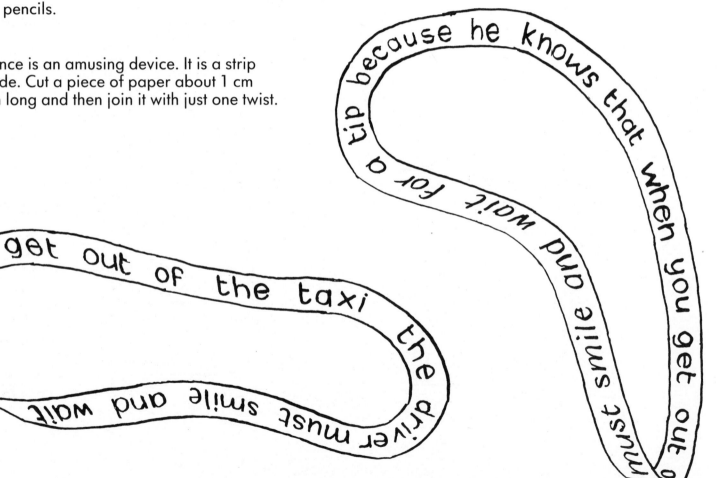

Family trees

Age range
Nine to eleven.

Group size
Whole class.

What you need
Examples of family trees, pencil and paper.

What to do
The nature of complex sentences can be interestingly demonstrated if you ask the children to construct a family tree, or you construct a large fictitious one yourself.

The class then have to describe the relationships within the family. For example, how many ways is it possible to describe James?
- James is Jenny's brother.
- Jo and Jean have four grandchildren of whom James is one.
- James is the great-grandson of Joseph Jones who was married to Jeanette Johnson who is thus James' great-grandmother.

John Jones = Janet

Jack = Janice Jarvice   Jane   Joseph = Jeanette Johnson

Joshua   Joanne = Jodie Jenkins   Joe = Jean Jackson

Julie = Jerry Jarman   Jacqueline   Judas Jennings = Judy   Jacob

Joan   Justin = Josie Jakes   James   Jenny   Jeffrey   Jolene = Julius Jardine

Jeremy   Jessica = Joel Jamerson   Jock   Jim Jordan = Joy   June

Jocelin   Jude   Jemima   Jill   Jerome   Johnathan

An alphabet of adjectives

Age range
Five to eleven.

Group size
Whole class.

What you need
Pencil and paper.

What to do
Ask the class to construct an alphabet of adjectives.
Start with a phrase of 'a' words and then substitute a
different adjective starting with 'b' and 'c' and so on. For
example:
    An amiable alligator
    A brown alligator
    A coughing alligator
    A dangerous alligator

Those children who are easily able to do this can then
be asked to construct an alphabet altering the adjective
and then the noun alternatively. For example:
    An amusing antelope
    A brown antelope
    A brown cougar
    A drowsy cougar
    A drowsy elephant.

Follow-up
If you know that your pupils can identify simple parts of
speech you could ask them to describe their morning in
adjectives only, or talk about a football match using
only verbs, eg running, shouting, kicking, straining,
leaping.

Substitutions

Age range
Seven to eleven.

Group size
Individuals or small groups.

What you need
Pencil and paper; a selection of activity pictures (Game 3).

What to do
This game allows children to explore sentence construction without supervision and without labels to learn. Start with a sentence containing the following:

Adjective	Subject	Verb	Object	Adverb
Pretty	girls	sing	songs	sadly

The sentences do not have to make sense. In fact children will probably prefer working with nonsense sentences. Words of a type can now be substituted to change the sentence until it undergoes a complete metamorphosis:

Fat girls sing songs sadly
Fat birds sing songs sadly
Fat birds sing songs loudly
Fat birds sing tunes loudly
White birds sing tunes loudly etc.

Game 2
Ask individuals or small groups to list nouns that relate to a specific topic eg domestic objects made of wood or yellow items in nature, with the intention of compiling the longest possible list.

Game 3
Give a group of children an evocative picture describing an activity eg a girl ice-skating, a motor-race etc. Then ask them for a list of related verbs like moving, speeding, competing etc.

moving
racing
skating
sliding
zooming

falling
laughing
slipping
speeding

Game 4
Ask one member of a group to act out an adverb while the rest of the class have to guess the correct word eg (crying) tearfully, (fighting) aggressively, (moving) slowly.

Game 5
Write a sentence with one nonsense word in it. For example:

She closed her eyes and plixed him.

Now get the children to find as many words as possible that will fit into the place of the nonsense word. For example:

She closed her eyes and kicked him.
shot him.
kissed him.

The substitute word must be the correct part of speech.

When the children are able to play this game, get them to invent their own words to place in a sentence.

Reconstructing sentences

Age range
Five to eleven.

Group size
Small groups.

What you need
Paper; scissors; pencils; newspaper (Game 2); card (Game 5).

What to do
These games will lead children to the realisation that words do what you want them to do, that they are not immutable, but can be móved about. Young children who begin to feel this kind of power in their use of words will feel able to edit, rearrange and develop their writing.

Game 1
Ask one child in the group to write down a sentence on a piece of paper without letting the rest of the group see what he has written. He then has to cut his sentence into single words and the rest of the group have to reconstruct the sentence.

Game 2
Choose an article from a newspaper, and ask the group of children to copy each sentence on to a separate slip of paper. After the slips have been shuffled the group has to make a new article by arranging the sentences in any order that makes sense. When they have finished they could compare it with the original and discuss the relative merits of each article.

Game 3

Get each group to write a meaningful sentence of about 25 words and then ask them to divide it up into three separate sentences (more words can be added at this stage to help if required). Then swap the three sentences with another group to be put back together into one sentence (leaving out one or two words if necessary).

Game 4

Ask each member of the group to write down a single word. The group's task is now to construct a sentence using each of the words that has been randomly presented to them. For example: John wrote cat. Brian wrote cries. Melanie wrote radio. Discussion between the group produced the sentence:

'If I force my cat to listen to the radio it cries.'

The game can be played with each member of the group writing two words, or even three if they become very proficient.

Game 5

Prepare simple sentences with each word on a separate card at least postcard size and preferably bigger. Give the children the word cards in random order and ask them to form a line so that the words read as a proper sentence. The game can be made easier by providing a capital letter at the front of the first word in the sentence, and a full stop to mark the final word.

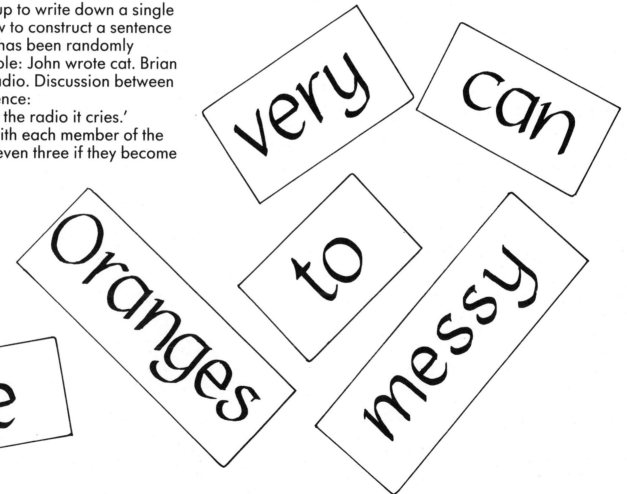

Adjectives for imagery

Age range
Seven to eleven.

Group size
Whole class.

What you need
List of nouns, pencil and paper.

What to do
Provide a list of nouns and ask the children to create an
evocative image by placing an adjective or adjectival
phrase with the given word.
    The wood = The dew-wet wood.
    Trees = Trees dripping with dew.
Or ask the children to make a list of possible endings to
go with the start of an image.
    A voice like . . .   ripe plums.
                          dead leaves.
                          a referee's whistle.
    Experiment with anthropomorphic imagery by asking
children to connect objects with imagery to do with
creatures.
    A tongue . . . like a slithering snake.
    Trees . . . like huge stalking giants.

The exquisite corpse

Age range
Nine to eleven.

Group size
Whole class.

What you need
Pencil and lined paper.

What to do
This game is a version of 'Consequences' and often results in phrases which have a surreal, bizarre quality.

Give each child a piece of paper on which are drawn several headed columns such as:

Adjective/Adjective/Noun/Verb/Adjective/Adjective/Noun

or

Adjective/Adjective/Noun/Verb/Adverb

The column headings stand for the main parts of speech required to make an interesting sentence. Give the children an explanation of these grammatical terms, but understanding will be strengthened by playing the game.

Each child writes down five adjectives in the first column and then folds the paper back so that the words cannot be seen. The paper is then handed on and five different adjectives are written in the second column (lined paper will ensure it is easy to read out the sentences at the end). This is folded back and passed on for five nouns to be written, and so on until each column has been filled. When the lists are completed, open out the paper and read out the resulting sentences across the page with definite or indefinite articles inserted where appropriate.

Adjective spinners

Age range
Five to eleven.

Group size
Pairs or small groups.

What you need
Card, matchstick, photocopiable page 118, pencil and paper, scissors.

What to do
For this game you will need to make sets of spinners. Patterns for these can be found on photocopiable page 118. Write six adjectives on each spinner. The adjectives should be appropriate to the age range and ability of the children. For example:

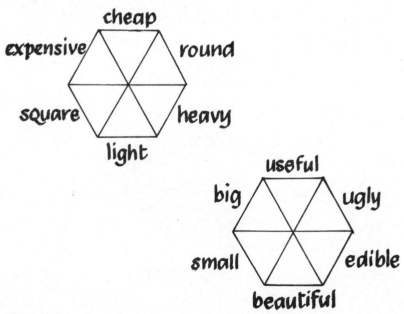

The spinner is more effective if it is made from card. Put a matchstick through the centre to spin it.

Give each group or pair of children two spinners. Spin them both at the same time. Write down the two words in the segment on which the spinners land (ie those closest to the table). Then ask the group to think of a noun which can be defined by the two adjectives. For example:

edible and expensive might be caviare or truffles
big and heavy – an elephant.

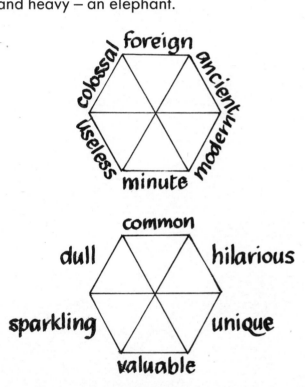

After a certain period of time ask the groups to come together and get one group to tell the other group its nouns. The second group then has to decide which two adjectives from the spinners were the ones matched to each noun.

Collecting comparisons

Age range
Seven to eleven.

Group size
Whole class.

What you need
Pictures like the ones shown here, pencil and paper.

What to do
Ask the children to look at these cartoons. Each picture is being compared to the others.

Then ask them to collect some words that give comparisons and try to draw cartoons to explain the words, as in the examples. Here are a few suggestions to start them off:

strong	stronger	strongest
tall	taller	tallest
fat	fatter	fattest
rich	richer	richest

small

smaller

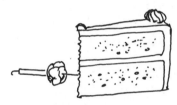

smallest

hairy

hairier

hairiest

Famous games and old favourites revised

There are many traditional games, TV and radio games that are based on word-play. These games survive and get handed on because they work and are fun to play. Many can be adapted for classroom use.

Charades

Age range
Five to eleven.

Group size
Whole class divided into groups of four or five children.

What you need
No specific requirements.

What to do
This game can be played in various ways and the most complex version, ie act out the title of a play, song, book or film, will test the ingenuity of the brightest child. For most children it is best to simplify the game, perhaps by asking groups of four or five to act out compound words like cowboy, sunflower, penknife, toothbrush, carpet etc. Each group will, of course, need time outside the room to discuss their plans before performing to the rest of the class.

Just a minute

Age range
Nine to eleven.

Group size
Whole class.

What you need
A list of prepared topics, stop-watch.

What to do
Ask individual pupils to talk for one minute without hesitation, repetition or deviation from a given subject to the rest of the class. This game will certainly be beyond the capability of young children but older children can play quite well if you choose suitable topics for them to talk about and act as a lenient referee.

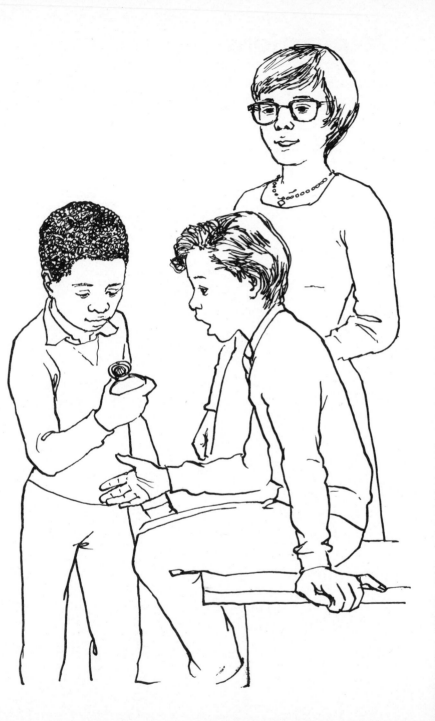

20 questions

Age range
Five to eleven.

Group size
Whole class.

What you need
No specific requirements.

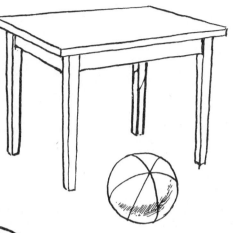

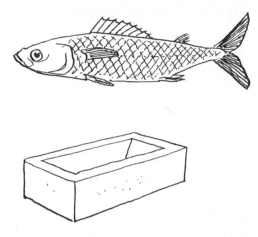

What to do

This is a classification game that has a number of possible variations. The most common form is where one child thinks of an object and declares it either 'animal', 'vegetable' or 'mineral', or a combination of these. Others are allowed to ask 20 questions which only demand a 'yes' or 'no' answer in an attempt to discover the identity of the object.

To simplify the game the target item could be more specifically identified before questions are asked. For example as one of a category of things such as an animal, or a book, or a form of transport, or a type of fruit, or a country. In an even more simple version, get groups of children to choose a subject eg breeds of dog, makes of car, breakfast cereal, types of shop etc. Each group then lists members of its chosen set for the others to guess the classification title. Alternatively you can announce a subject title and ask the children in turn to name individual examples.

What's my line?

Age range
Five to eleven.

Group size
Whole class.

What you need
No specific requirements.

What to do
In 'What's my line?' one pupil pretends to have a
particular occupation eg fireman, nurse, actress,
computer programmer etc which the rest of the class
has to discover by asking questions that demand 'yes'
or 'no' answers.

Hangman

Age range
Seven to eleven.

Group size
Whole class divided into large groups.

What you need
Pencil and paper.

What to do
Hangman is an age-old favourite that now has computer versions. It is still useful for the opportunity it allows for discussion about the likelihood of certain letters preceding or following others. The children have to guess a word, represented by dashes, one letter at a time. Wrong guesses result in one line being added to the diagram of a gibbet and the incorrect letter being written, as a reminder, on a separate line. The children have to guess the word before they are hung.

Since there are 26 letters in the alphabet a diagram of 12 lines gives the players roughly a 2 to 1 chance of being correct. If the effect of having two of the same letter in one word is taken into account as well as the fact that only certain letter combinations are likely, it becomes even easier to 'win'. To increase the difficulty therefore one has to draw a very simple diagram!

For young children who have difficulty with the game it is sometimes useful to stipulate that the words must be the names of children within the class. Later they could move on to names of famous characters in books or on television, or book titles, before being allowed a completely free choice of words.

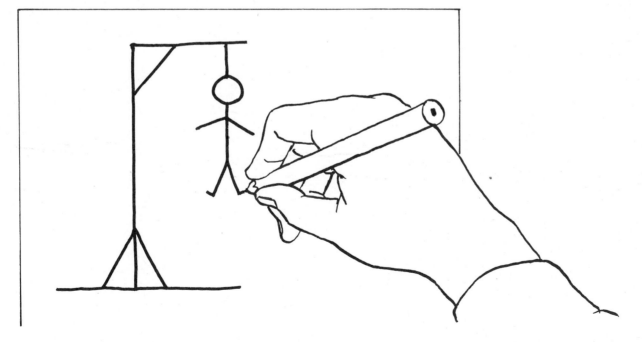

I went to market

Age range
Five to nine.

Group size
Large group sitting in a circle.

What you need
No specific requirements.

What to do
Most children will know this game from a very young age. The first child in the circle adds a word to the sentence: 'I went to market and bought', the second adds another word to the list having repeated the first one, and so on until the last child has the whole list of words to remember.

The game is actually easier if each succeeding object has to start with the next letter of the alphabet, so start with apples and then biscuits, coconuts etc.

Crosswords

Age range
Five to eleven.

Group size
Individuals.

What you need
A variety of crosswords, a dictionary, pencil and paper, photocopiable pages 119 and 120.

What to do
Crosswords engage people of all ages and abilities. When they are used with children care must be taken that the technical and vocabulary levels are suitable.

For young children a sufficient introduction to crosswords is provided by simple clues allied to words where each letter is represented by a dash. For example:

It barks _ _ _

It has leaves _ R _ _

Something that carries you over the sea S _ _ _

The next stage is to use very simple four and five word crosswords.

Clues down: 1 Large with leaves
3 Catch fish in this

Clues across 2 Queen's hat
4 Worn round the neck

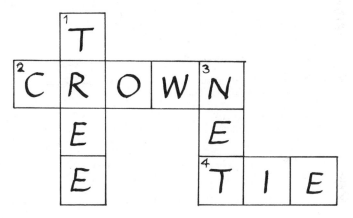

Picture clues can also be used

Clues down

1

3

Clues across

2

4

Older children will enjoy designing their own crosswords ie filling a ten by ten square grid with as many interlocking words as possible and then colouring the blanks black. Afterwards they can provide clues for their friends to use in solving the puzzle. (It's a good idea to ask children to check their words in a dictionary before handing on the crossword to be solved.) The advantage of these crosswords is that they will be constructed at the level of the children who attempt to solve them.

You could also photocopy some blank crossword grids for the children to fill in, using photocopiable pages 119 and 120.

Some children will enjoy collecting simple crosswords from daily newspapers and sticking them into a crossword book.

Donkey

Age range
Seven to eleven.

Group size
Small groups.

What you need
Pencil and paper.

What to do
Donkey is another well-known game that can aid spelling through encouraging an awareness of letter combinations.

One of the group writes down a letter. The next child follows the first letter with another to start to make a word. The third child adds another letter to the word but does not finish it. So each child adds a letter to the potential word without completing it. For example:

Mike writes 'b'
Sarah writes 'o'
Sally writes 'o'

Sam can't think of another letter to keep the word going and so is 'out'. 'K', 'm', 'n', 'r', and 't' finish the word, but Sam could have chosen 'z' thinking of the word 'booze' or 's' thinking of the word 'boost'.

A player cannot be counted out on a three letter word and any player can challenge the person before him if he thinks that the letter given makes any word impossible. Of course the challenger himself goes out if the challenged player can declare a genuine word.

Snap and bingo

Age range
Five to eleven.

Group size
Small groups or whole class.

What you need
Snap and bingo cards.

What to do
The traditional game of snap using words and pictures on card will familiarise children with the spelling of words that the teacher thinks are needed by particular children. For example words that young children frequently use in their writing or technical words currently being used as part of a topic. For older children the pack could contain words with spelling peculiarities such as receive, cough, comb etc. Obviously these packs would need to be added to or changed regularly if they were to retain their usefulness.

skull
spine
knuckle
scalp
knee
ankle
stomach
wrist
should

aeroplane
omnibus
vehicle
toboggan
submarine
glider
yacht
bicycle
carriage

Word bingo can be played by all age groups, using a board that contains nine or so words and matching 'flash cards' with either you or a child as the 'caller'. With younger children the caller should show as well as say the word. Players mark off the words on their cards as they are called out until they have a full card, with the winner having to read off his words for the caller to check. Cards could perhaps be prepared around a current interest, eg names for parts of the body: skull, spine, scalp, knuckle etc. Or prepare cards based on a particular book, or on different word families. With this game, as with many others, encourage the children to become involved in designing the game rather than just presenting them with it. At the very least the children could draw illustrations on the cards to make them more attractive and interesting.

Dominoes

Age range
Five to eleven.

Group size
Small groups.

What you need
Photocopiable pages 121 and 122, card, scissors, adhesive.

What to do
Dominoes is a game that can be adapted to your particular purpose. The format has any number of variations. For example:

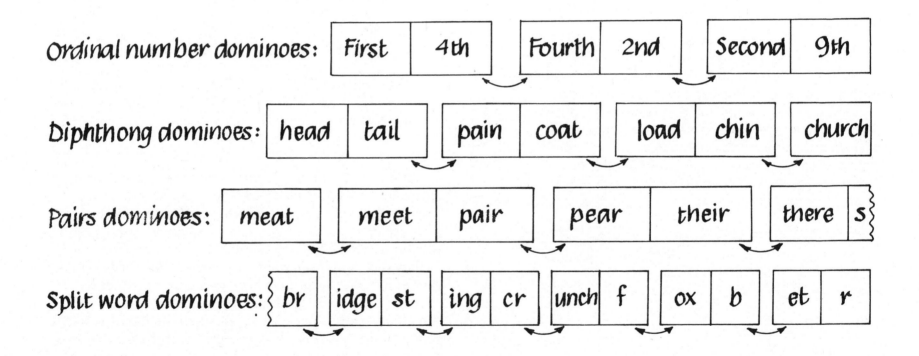

Ordinal number dominoes: | First | 4th | Fourth | 2nd | Second | 9th

Diphthong dominoes: | head | tail | pain | coat | load | chin | church

Pairs dominoes: | meat | meet | pair | pear | their | there | s

Split word dominoes: | br | idge | st | ing | cr | unch | f | ox | b | et | r

Use the photocopiable sheets (on pages 121 and 122) which can be cut and stuck on to card to make a set of ordinal dominoes.

Letter logic

Age range
Nine to eleven.

Group size
Pairs.

What you need
Pencil and paper.

What to do

A player chooses a four letter word and writes it down but does not show it to his opponent. His opponent by a series of guesses and deductions has to arrive at this word. For example: Player 1 writes G A V E. Player 1 will now use a set of symbols to match Player 2's guess against this word:

  ★   Star = the correct letter is earlier in the alphabet.
  △   Triangle = the correct letter occurs later in the alphabet.
  †   Cross = this a correct letter in the wrong place.
  ✓   Tick = this is the right letter in the right place.

So if Player 2 writes G O A T, Player 1 would place his clues under the word thus G O A T
                          ✓★†★

Player 2 may deduce from this that the correct word may be G A T E so Player 1 will again mark his clues G A T E and so on until the correct answer is arrived at.
✓✓△✓

Coffee pot

Age range
Five to eleven.

Group size
Whole class.

What you need
No specific requirements.

What to do
The simplest version of this game is to ask one child to think of an object and the others to ask questions to discover the name of that object. For example: 'How big is your coffee pot?', 'Is your coffee pot in this room?', 'What is your coffee pot made of?'.

Game 2
This is a more difficult version which is likely to be successful only with more able children. One child is the player and leaves the room while the rest of the group chooses a word, preferably one that is flexible in meaning, which the player then has to guess. The player returns and asks individuals in the group questions.

  The replies have to include the 'secret' word, but 'coffee pot' is substituted for it. So if the word was 'saw/sore' the game might work as follows:

Player: What day is it today?
Answer: I coffee pot it was Monday on the calendar.
Player: What's the weather like?
Answer: Hot. I coffee pot the sun shining this morning.
Player: Why are you wearing a jumper if it is hot?
Answer: Well it stops me getting coffee pot shoulders from sunburn.

The best words for this game are common verbs such as: see, like, hate, make, say etc.

Game 3
In this version half the children leave the room, while those remaining choose a verb. When the other children return, they are given a word that rhymes with the chosen one. From this information, they have to try to guess the chosen word but instead of saying what they think it is, they have to silently act out their guess. If they guess correctly, they are applauded; if they fail, they are hissed. This goes on until the correct word is guessed.

Call my bluff

Age range
Nine to eleven.

Group size
Groups of three children.

What you need
Dictionary, pencil and paper.

A dish of mixed ingredients

A 19th Century bicycle

A playground game

Hotchpotch

What to do
Divide the class into groups of three and give them time to prepare. Using a large dictionary ask them to find a word that is so obscure that other groups will not know its meaning. Then all three in each group have to write a short definition of the word, only one of which is correct.

To play the game the opposing groups have to guess which of the given definitions is the correct one. Ingenuity, and good acting, is required in order to make the false definitions seem more plausible than the true one.

Hunting for words

Children are amused by linguistic oddities. They are intrigued by the sounds and shapes of words. If children are considering words as interesting things in themselves, and they are concerned about words and find them worth collecting, then they are moving a considerable way towards competence in language, for competence cannot be achieved without a prior interest.

The games in this section are intended to encourage in children an awareness of the variety of language and to extend their vocabulary. Children will enjoy collecting words and using them in new and interesting ways, but only if they are helped by a sensitive teacher. As with many of the games in this book those in this section can be used to create pleasure and excitement and to encourage a lively and inventive use of language.

Most of the games and activities in this section will result in collections of words. Such collections could be kept in a variety of 'home-made' books in a corner of the classroom: long thin books, short fat books, giant-size books, square or triangular-shaped books, and concertina books.

Or ask your pupils to make a row of decorated boxes for different word families:

There are of course various ways of displaying your word collections. Perhaps build a brick wall display with the new words that the class collects:

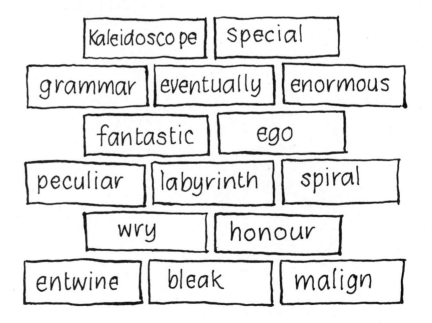

Or devise a collecting point that matches the words. For instance, an infant class could make circular pockets out of card large enough to take small word cards, and then give each pocket an expression. Appropriate adjectives can then be placed in the relevant pocket.

A simple idea for a wall dictionary is to let the children paint a bright circular sun. Prepare 26 rays out of thin strips of card. Then put the rays, one for each letter of the alphabet, in position so that they radiate from the sun and can be extended as new words are discovered and recorded.

joyful

pleased

sad

mournful

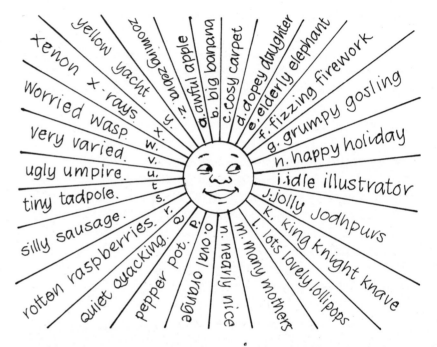

worried

angry

Although the games in this section specify particular word-hunting activities, hunting for and collecting words can start from almost any point.

Collecting ambiguous signs and notices is a light-hearted way of inviting children to look carefully at the language around them. For example: St John's Drive In or Stop Children Crossing.

Collecting advertisement words also promotes thought about precise word usage. What, for instance, does 'fresh' mean when applied to a tube of toothpaste?

Many children have hobbies which involve them collecting items such as coins, stamps and badges. These collections can be used as the starting point for hunting and collecting words.

- Stickers, for instance, can provoke discussion about any number of topics. They can lead into searches for more information, and can be integrated into larger word collections.
- Labels, especially those from food cartons and cans provide an endless source of discussion about ingredients, countries of origin, graphic design etc.
- Postcard collections can be used to stimulate a class collection so that children add to it by writing from their holiday locations, or by bringing back postcard souvenirs from visits to museums and other places of interest.
- Programmes from football matches, exhibitions, concerts etc can be used to encourage comment and discussion about words and can be used to lead into such work as writing and designing programmes, perhaps for some genuine forthcoming school event. All these sources can be used as the basis of word

collections as can specialist dictionaries, eg *The Oxford Dictionary of English Place Names* (Oxford University Press), thesauri and encyclopaedias. Some children will enjoy making lists of unusual names by thumbing through a telephone directory, others will enjoy collecting interesting words by looking through poetry anthologies. So as well as playing the word-hunting games, make other collections of slang, clichés, proverbs, playground rhymes, riddles and jokes. Put them in books with cartoons, paintings, magazine pictures, photographs and sketches and have them in the classroom for the children to enjoy.

Making lists

Age range
Five to seven.

Group size
Whole class.

What you need
Pencil and paper; a few simple poems (Game 2); dictionaries (Game 3).

What to do
There are many activities that can be based on the writing of lists. For instance lists can make a simple poetic form. All sorts of lists can be a good starting point for this, from shopping lists – a poor person's shopping list set against a rich person's; or a country list compared to a town list; or a man's compared to a woman's; or a fantasy list – to lists with titles such as 'Things I like' or 'Reasons to be cheerful'.

Things I like:
1. Skate boarding
2. Top of the Pops
3. Comics
4. Eating tea
5. Football
6. Swimming
7.
8.

Game 1
Many lists are best introduced orally and then written down later for reference such as lists of antonyms (an antonym is a word opposite in meaning to another). If you start exploring simple examples of opposites, you will find it will not be long before you move into areas where the answers are not so easy or where there might be more than one acceptable answer. Is the opposite of weak, powerful or strong? One way of dealing with this, apart from via discussion, is by writing clusters of words on the blackboard and asking the children to write a collection of antonyms. For example:

If you introduce a competitive element and ask groups of children to write lists then the effort to write the longest list, will inevitably lead children to experiment. Lists of colours may include such items as 'grey-green' and 'sunshiny'. Phrases may start to appear, eg 'sort of blue with speckles of grey'. Prized words and phrases can be put on display.

More formally, you could provide a list of adjectives, such as words referring to qualities of texture – plush, sharp, squelchy, gnarled – and ask the children to provide appropriate nouns. Here though some discussion will again be necessary in order to explore the suitability of certain collections. Is soft sandpaper valid?

Game 2

Simple poems are often lists and can provide interesting formats for language play. For example:

> **Have you ever seen?**
>
> Have you ever seen
> a blue tadpole
> Have you ever seen
> a spoilt-brat toad
>
> Have you ever seen
> a walking fish
> Have you ever seen
> a grunting chick
>
> Have you ever seen
> a singing spider
> Have you ever seen
> a dancing tiger
>
> Have you ever seen
> a monkey swimming
> Have you ever seen
> a turtle grinning
>
> Have you ever?
>
> Grace Nichols

Using this poem as a model, children could write their own 'Have you seen' list.

Game 3

Colour is obviously very much a part of our lives, but colour words don't simply describe, they symbolise and are often found in combination with other words. Ask the children to use a dictionary to find colour word combinations and phrases. Get each child to make a list in which only one example of each colour is allowed and then pass it to a partner to find the definitions. Such a list might include white lie, blackmail, red tape, yellow streak, green room, orangery, out of the blue etc.

Twin words

Age range
Nine to eleven.

Group size
Whole class.

What you need
Pencil and paper, dictionaries.

What to do
Ask the children to search for strange sounding twin-words that are not like everyday words and find their meanings in the dictionary. Some of these words are so old that the original reason for them has been lost in time.

In some twin-words the second half rhymes with the first.

humdrum

hugger-mugger

harum-scarum

hotchpotch

helter-skelter

In others there is no rhyme but both words start with the same letter, and often end in a similar way . . . .

ping-pong

riff-raff

pitter-patter

tittle-tattle

dilly-dally

Biggest and best

Age range
Five to eleven.

Group size
Pairs or small groups.

What you need
Pencil and paper, stop-watch.

What to do
This is a word-hunting activity which can, if you wish, become a competition between pairs or groups of children. Ask the children to work with a partner to see if they can write a list of words for the largest things in the world. For example:

Skyscrapers – the tallest buildings in the world.
Oceans – the largest masses of water in the world.
Whales – the largest creatures in the sea.

Can they write a word list for the smallest things in the world like droplet or microbe?

Then ask them to try to write a list of words that mean biggest, or best.

Additional lists might be:
- Words for small, like tiny, microscopic etc.
- Words for short or fat things like stubby, squat etc.
- Words for long or thin things like thread, sliver etc.
- Words which describe graceful movements like glide and drift.
- Words which describe struggling movements like thrash and bustle.
- Make a list of beautiful things, beautiful creatures, flowers, places.

After a previously agreed time limit, each pair or

group counts the numbers of words in its list to determine the winners.

Follow-up
To encourage children to word-hunt for information and use 'popular fact' books, organise a game in terms of names for the biggest and best ie:

What is the name of the largest ocean, the biggest whale, the tallest skyscraper etc?

Sound words

Age range
Seven to eleven.

Group size
Pairs.

What you need
Comics, scissors, adhesive, pencil and paper.

What to do
The use of onomatopoeia (words whose sound helps to suggest the meaning) is an important element in a lot of poetry. One way of introducing children to this feature of language is to show them words in comics which are used to imitate a sound.

Get the children to go through comics and make a list of all the words, or cut them out and stick them on paper.

Ask them to think of other words that imitate a sound. Animal noises very often do:

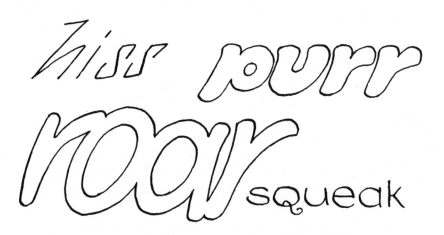

Suggest that they work with a partner to see which pair can collect the most sound words.

Collecting names

Age range
Five to eleven.

Group size
Whole class divided into groups.

What you need
Pencil and paper.

What to do
Ask the children to find the most popular names for boys and girls in your school by conducting a survey and then perhaps making a graph of what they find.

Suggest to the children that they collect names and keep them in lists:
- Their favourite boys' or girls' names.
- Names of Kings and Queens.
- Names of pop groups.
- Names of football players.
- Names of television characters.
- Names of birds.

Provide the children with the names of various characters from stories, rhymes and films. Ask them to add to the list:
Willie Wonka
King Kong
Rumpelstiltskin
Winnie-the-Pooh
Gumdrop
Tarzan
Augustus Gloop
Dr Who
Frankenstein
Superman
Dracula
Humpty Dumpty
Albert Herbert Hawkins
(the naughtiest boy in
the world).

Then perhaps, the groups could, in discussion, invent imaginary explanations of how these characters got their names and report their explanations to the class.

Shape words

Age range
Nine to eleven.

Group size
Pairs.

What you need
Examples of shape words, pencil and paper.

What to do
Provide the children with some examples of words that have been made into a little picture of their meaning. For example:

Then ask the children to collect some words like this and make a drawing of them. It may be that the children will find the activity easier if they work with a partner, so that conversation sparks ideas.

A grouping game

Age range
Five to eleven.

Group size
Pairs.

What you need
Pencil and paper.

What to do
You will need to introduce this game in stages with instructions like the following:

- Look carefully at the lists given.
- Can you add a word at the end of each line to name the group?
  Guitar, flute, trumpet, drum, violin, harp are all . . .
  Italy, Canada, Australia, India, Israel are all . . .
  Rose, daffodil, bluebell, pansy, geranium are all . . .
- Make up your own lists to go with the following nouns: furniture, clothes, fruit, sports, television characters.
- Now sit with a friend and play this game. You start the game by saying to your friend . . . 'I'm thinking of vegetables and the first one is carrot' or 'I'm thinking of toys and the first one is a skipping rope'. Your friend has to add the next word to the list and then you have to add the next and so on. See how long you can make your lists. You mustn't repeat any item.
  You lose if you can't think of a word to add to the list within an agreed time.

Puns

Age range
Seven to eleven.

Group size
Whole class.

What you need
Pencil and paper.

What to do
Some puns, such as those shown here derive from homophones (words which have the same sound but different meanings):

Which fruit always comes in twos?
Pears (pairs)!
Which number never loses?
One (won)!
Other puns are based on one word which has a variety of meanings.

I get a kick out of you!

The easiest way to help the children to invent puns is by asking them first to make a list of words which sound the same but have different meanings such as: see, sea; meat, meet; pane, pain; mussels, muscles; knows, nose; boy, buoy; ewe, you. Then ask them to make up riddles based on the homophones:

Which animal never wears clothes?
A Bear (Bare)!

Alphabet feast

Age range
Five to nine.

Group size
Whole class.

What you need
The alphabet, pencil and paper.

What to do
Tell the children that they are going to plan a feast! This is an alphabet feast, though, which means they have to select foods in alphabetical order.

Begin with A – what will they choose?
Apples? Or perhaps anchovies?

Next B . . .
Bread? Or butter? Or beer?

Now what will they choose for C? and for D?
Explain that it might be difficult to discover foods for Q and X. Perhaps they could find something to decorate the alphabet feast table that begins with Q and X.

Animal menus

Age range
Five to nine.

Group size
Individuals.

What you need
Thin card, scissors, felt-tipped pens, books on animals.

What to do
Ask the children to write a menu for a restaurant where alligators eat.

What about a menu for a restaurant where bats and beasties eat?

Variation
Ask the children to make up a menu that shows the *real* diet of an animal or bird and then show that menu to a friend to see if the menu gives enough clues to the animal in question to make it identifiable. Some research might be needed here!

Hidden words

Age range
Five to eleven.

Group size
Whole class.

What you need
Examples of hidden words, pencil and paper.

What to do
Sometimes short words hide inside long ones. Each of the long words given here has at least one short word hiding inside it. Give these as examples and ask the children to find the hidden words.

another

attention

mathematical

problem

orange

vegetables

hippopotamus

students

decorate

Get the children to collect long words that have short words hiding inside and show their list to a friend to see if they can pick out the words in disguise.

Word webs

Age range
Seven to eleven.

Group size
Small groups.

What you need
Key words, pencil and paper, photocopiable
pages 123 and 124, dictionaries or thesauri (optional).

What to do
A useful way of helping children to understand how the
context of words can affect their meaning is to draw a
word web.

Write a key word in the centre of a page and then
give it to a group of children and ask them to write
around it all the associated words they can think of, eg
the word EYE appears in many lexical sets.

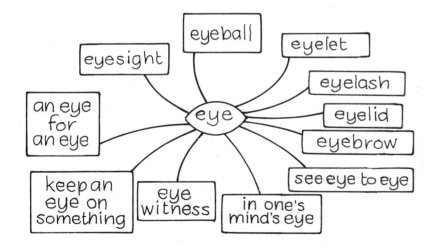

Keep these diagrams and the children can add to
them as they learn new words and phrases. Older
children can be asked to colour-code the web, red for
verbs, blue for nouns, yellow for phrases, sayings etc.
The following are suggested 'starter' words:

   table   look   happy   laugh   head

Older children can make use of a thesaurus such as
The Word Hunter's Companion: A First Thesaurus edited
by James Green (Basil Blackwell).

Game 2
Word webs can occur in a variety of forms. They can be
used to do some work on synonyms. (Synonyms are
words which sound different but have the same meaning
eg jumper and sweater.) For example, put 'said' in the
middle of a page and ask how many synonyms the
children can find. An alternative format is to write the
replacements for 'said' in a speech bubble.

Or, if the word was 'walk', in a foot:

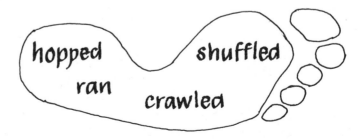

Or make verb webs. Provide a picture, say of a footballer, and ask the children to make a web which expresses all the things a footballer might do during a game of football.

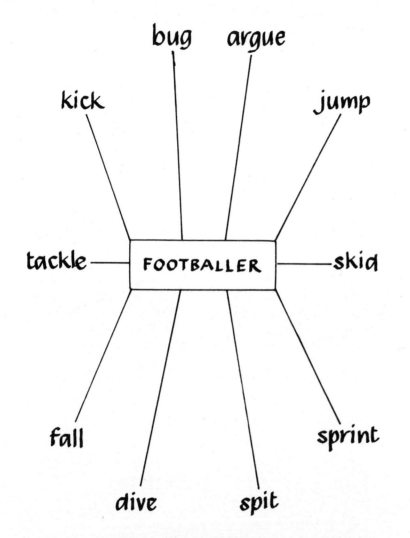

An empty speech bubble and foot are provided on pages 123 and 124 for photocopying.

Game 3

A similar diagrammatic activity can be done using familiar collations, the kind of groupings that occur in word association exercises. Word families can be built up on the blackboard as a class activity or you could provide a key word for groups of children to build on.

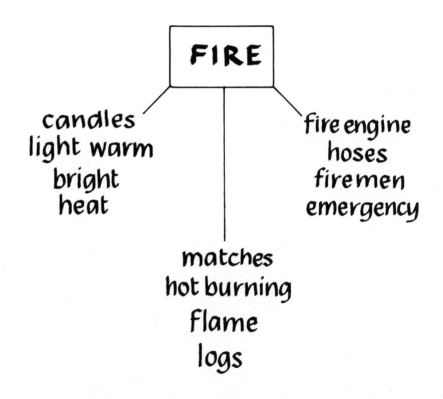

The children will obviously have to decide which words to add to the diagram, where to place them, which words link with which and why etc. This sort of discussion will generate thinking about the meaning of words and their relationships. Again, a good children's thesaurus or dictionary will be useful.

Word trees

Age range
Seven to eleven.

Group size
Small groups.

What you need
Photocopiable page 125, pencil and paper.

What to do
One way to collect words together in groups, is to show groups of words in a diagram that looks like a tree. Each of the branches can be as long as you like, of course. And you can add as many branches as you wish. Your tree might be very complex.

Start the activity by providing subjects such as games, transport, occupations, buildings etc. Then get the groups of children to make up word trees of their own. Some children might prefer to work on an empty tree diagram. A photocopiable skeleton tree is provided on page 125.

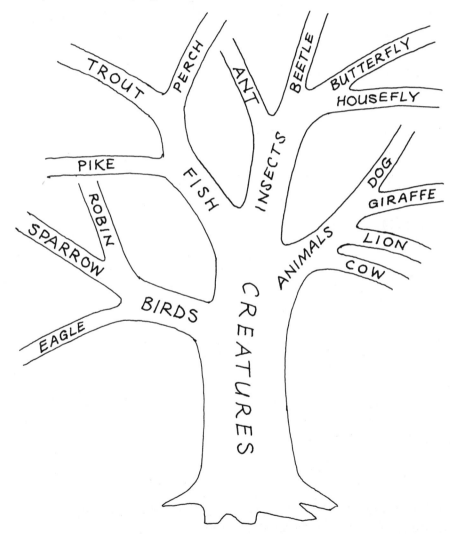

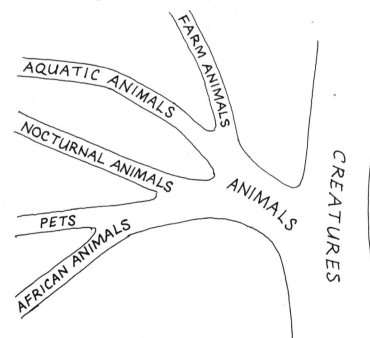

Kill the don't

Age range
Five to eleven.

Group size
Whole class.

What you need
Examples of don'ts, card, scissors, felt-tipped pens.

'Don't talk in assembly!'

What to do
As a class, make a collection of 'don'ts', such as:
- School don'ts': Don't run in the corridors.
- Home 'don'ts': Don't jump on the sofa.
- Odd 'don'ts': Don't pick your nose.

Then let the children try to turn the 'don'ts' into positive messages in order to try to make unpopular 'don'ts' more acceptable; ie kill the don't. String 'don'ts' cards across the room with the alternative positive message on the other side. Have 'don'ts' illustrated in cartoons with speech balloons.

Organise the 'don'ts' in various ways. For example, in order of popularity or in order of justifiability of the rule. Ask the children to write out a set that they would want to teach to their brother or sister, or their parents.

Word partners

Age range
Nine to eleven.

Group size
Pairs.

What you need
Reference books, pencil and paper.

What to do
Give each member of the pair a set length of time to write down either the male or female version of an animal or human. For example: duck (drake), fox (vixen), witch (warlock), queen (king) etc.

At the end of the allocated time, ask the children to swap lists, and by using whatever books are available (but not by asking the teacher!) each child has to find the partner words to the ones on their list.

The game can be played with a variety of categories:
Home words: rabbit/warren   vicar/vicarage
Countries/capitals: London/England   Paris/France
Parents/offspring: sheep/lamb   duck/duckling
Collective nouns: netballers/team   sheep/flock

Inventing names

Age range
Five to eleven.

Group size
Whole class.

What you need
Name lists, pencil and paper.

What to do
Discuss with the children how they would set about choosing a new name. Perhaps they would choose different names depending on the sort of person they were, or what sort of job they did. Ask them to make up their own names for some of the following:

An evil character.

A very old person.

A tramp.

A greedy person.

A pop star.

A nosy neighbour.

A creature from another planet.

A farmer.

A robot.

A magician.

A very rich person.

A racing driver.

A fashion model.

A lorry driver.

A sailor.

A shy person.

A teacher.

Ask the older children to write a brief character sketch to go with each name.

Can they make up good nicknames for different animals? What nicknames would they give to: a hedgehog, a polar bear, a lion, a kangaroo, a donkey, a pig, a giraffe, a walrus, a tiger, an elephant, a goose, a fox.

Word pictures

Age range
Five to eleven.

Group size
Whole class.

What you need
Examples of word pictures, pencil and paper.

What to do
What word does this picture make you think of?

What word do you think this is a picture of?

What word does this picture give a clue to?

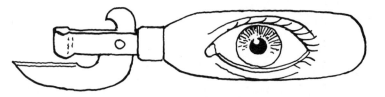

You will find that the children will collect lots of word pictures like this once they get started. Ask them to draw a funny picture of a word and then show it to a friend to see if they can guess the word. Provide some funny picture words to start them off . . . .

pancake

tablespoon

football

clock-tower

walking stick

bookcase

penknife

eyelid

Dictionary searches

Age range
Seven to eleven.

Group size
Small groups.

What you need
Dictionaries, pencil and paper.

What to do
One way of helping the children to become familiar with a dictionary is to send them off on a word hunt.

Ask small groups of children to find:

- one letter words
- two letter words
- three letter words
- four letter words etc

until they get 'stuck'.

Hunt for words that don't include one of the five vowels a, e, i, o, u.

Hunt for words that don't contain two vowels in alphabetical order, eg 'a' then 'e'.

Hunt for a word that contains three vowels in alphabetical order, then four.

Hunt for a word that contains all five vowels eg facetious.

Try to discover some palindromes ie words that can be spelt the same way forwards and backwards.

Hunt for a word that it is easy/impossible to begin/end sentences with.

Hunt for a word that doesn't make sense after 'I'.

Hunt for a word that does/doesn't make sense after 'the'.

Hunt for a word that can be turned into a negative by adding a sound or syllable eg happy/unhappy.

Hunt for words that start with an unusual combination of letters eg 'gno' as in gnocchi, 'rh' as in rhapsody, 'xy' as in xylophone. What do the words with the funny beginnings mean.

Find words with funny endings.

Find all the words that begin with 'a' that are made up of shorter words eg alliteration gives all, lit, rat, ion, on and ration. Then try the same thing using 'b'.

Find some compound words, ie words that are made up of other shorter words like lighthouse, wristwatch, teapot, postman, football, penknife.

Thesaurus searches

Age range
Nine to eleven.

Group size
Whole class.

What you need
Children's thesauri (see page 126), pencil and paper.

What to do
A thesaurus even more than a dictionary can open our eyes to the possibilities and varieties of words (thesauri for young children are recommended on page 126).

One way of getting children to start using a thesaurus is to ask them to create complex wordy versions of simple phrases using unusual words culled from thesauri. You could start by expressing some of your normal classroom directions in an elaborate way, for example:

'Sit in a circle' could be 'Please move yourselves into a conchoidal arrangement of bodies in repose'. 'I suggest you commence forming yourselves into a undeviating line by the wooden exit', translates as 'Make a straight line by the door'.

Then ask the children to devise long-winded phrases for their friends to translate.

Of course, the children mustn't be left with the impression that elaborate sentences are necessary for good writing.

Yellow pages

Age range
Seven to eleven.

Group size
Small groups.

What you need
Yellow Pages telephone directory, pencil and paper.

What to do
This is another game which requires a book search to find information, use an index and practice using alphabetical order. Working in groups, get the children to set each other problems which can be solved by reference to the *Yellow Pages* telephone directory. Give them some examples to start with such as the following:
- You break a window when your parents are out. Can you find someone to mend it before they get back? (Answer: the name and number of an emergency glazier.)

- You have missed the last bus home at night. It is too far to walk. What are you to do? (Answer: a 24 hour taxi service.)
- You don't know how much money to take with you to pay the entry to the swimming baths. How do you find out? (Answer: The reception telephone number of the local swimming baths.)

When the groups are satisfied with their answers, get them to return to the group which set the problem for checking.

Reproducible material

Word machines, see page 18

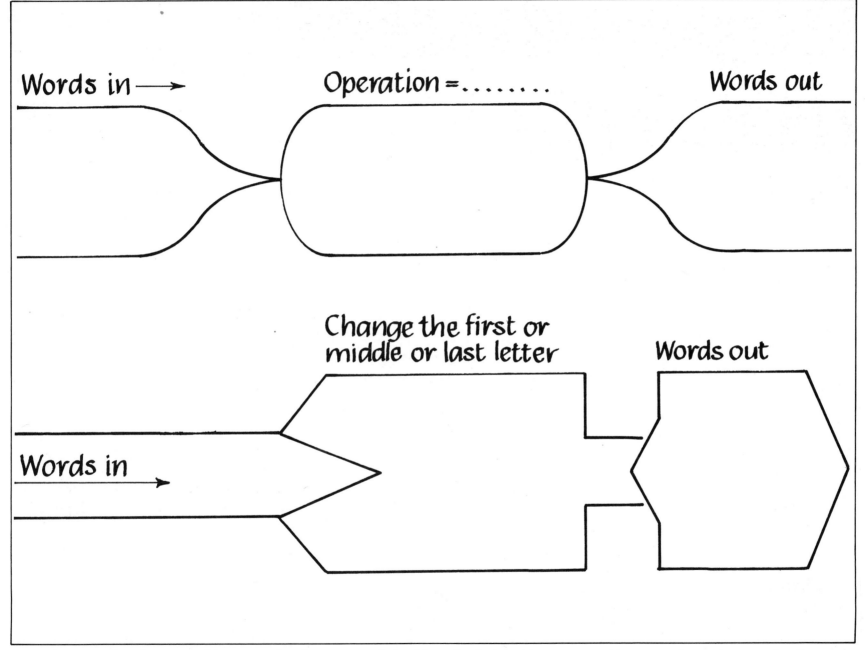

Words in →

Operation = ...

Words out

Change the first or middle or last letter

Words out

Words in →

Word machines, see page 18

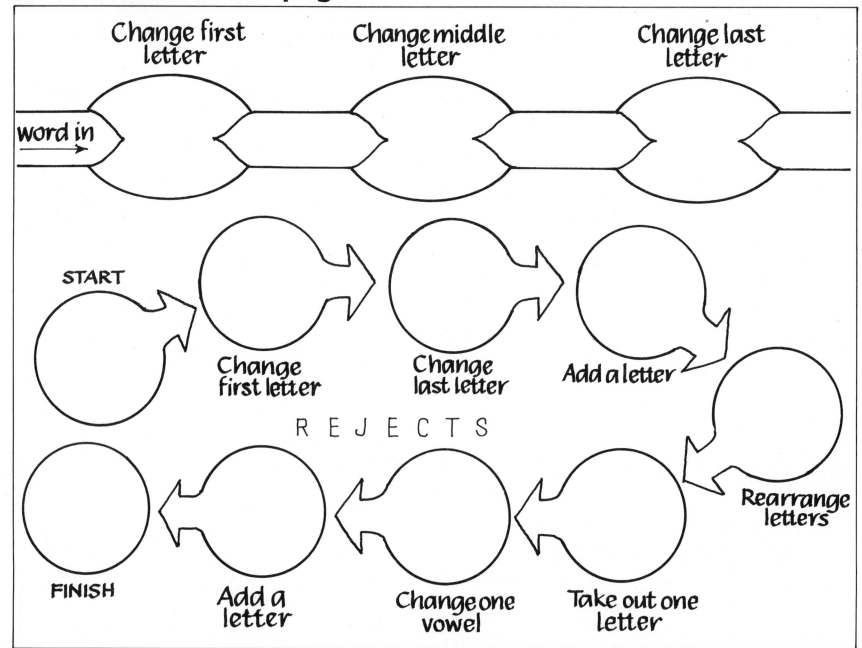

Word matrices, see page 20

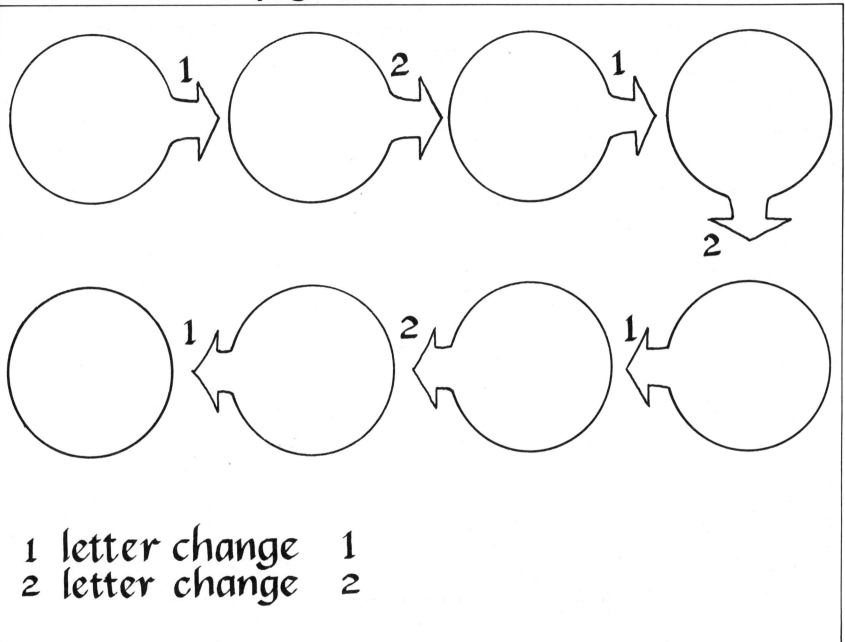

1 letter change   1
2 letter change   2

Word matrices, see page 20

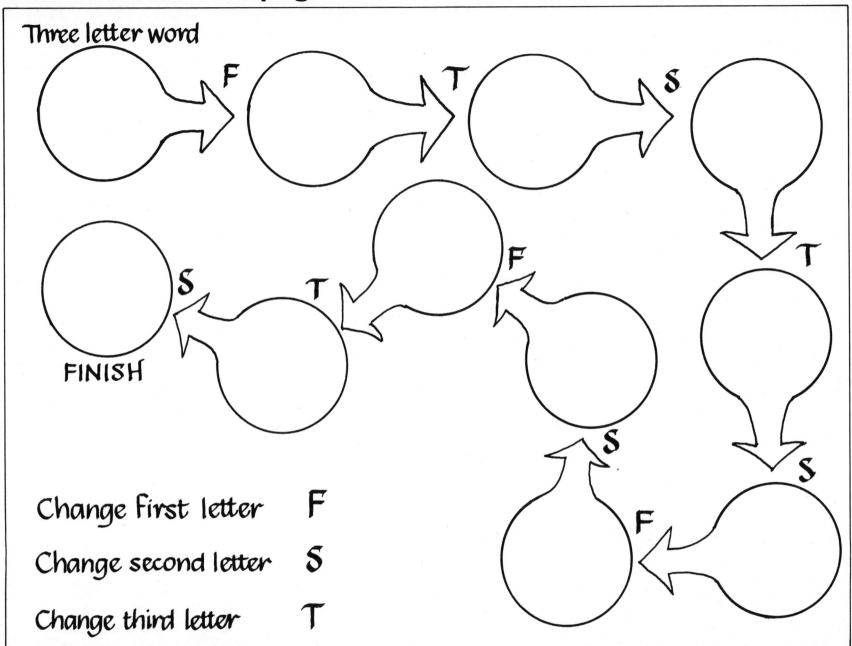

Three letter word

F → T → S → T → S → F → T → S (FINISH)

Change first letter   F

Change second letter   S

Change third letter   T

Word matrices, see page 20

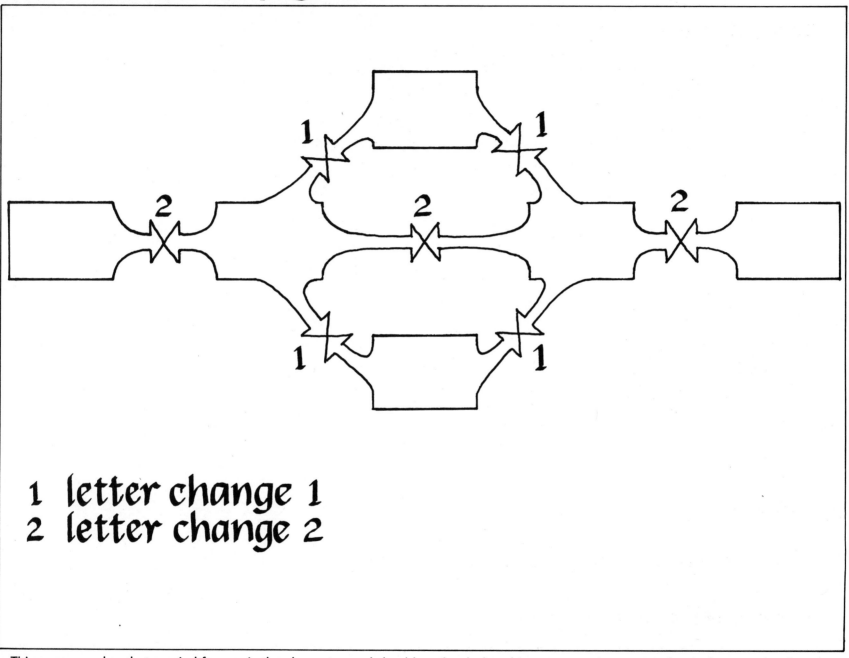

1 **letter change** 1
2 **letter change** 2

Word matrices, see page 20

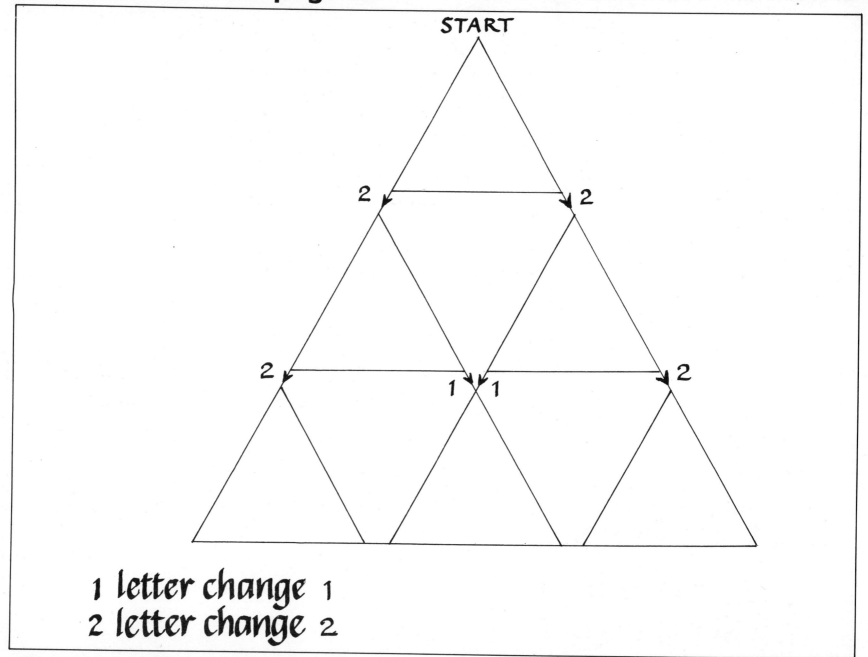

START

2 letter change 2
1 letter change 1

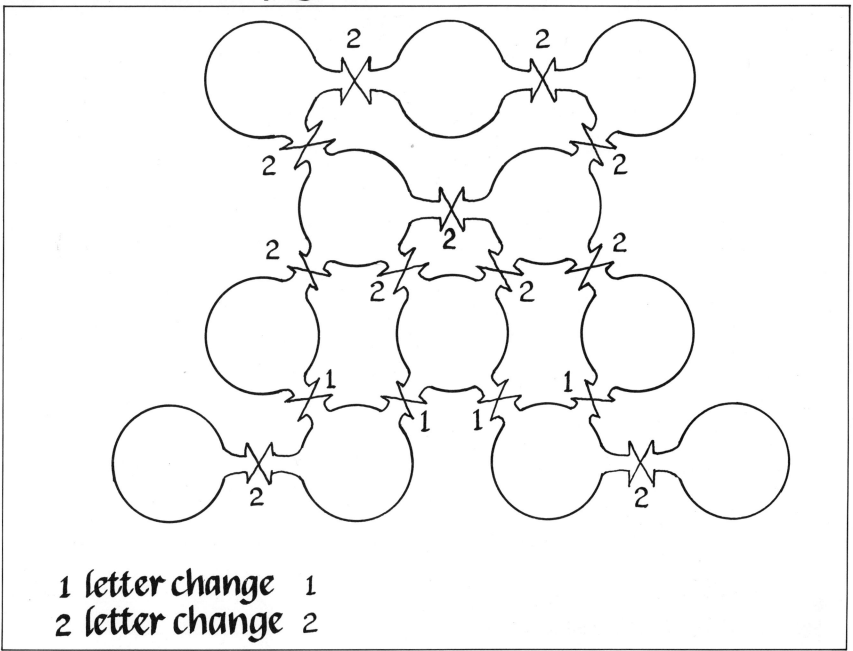

1 letter change   1
2 letter change   2

Gameboards, see page 29

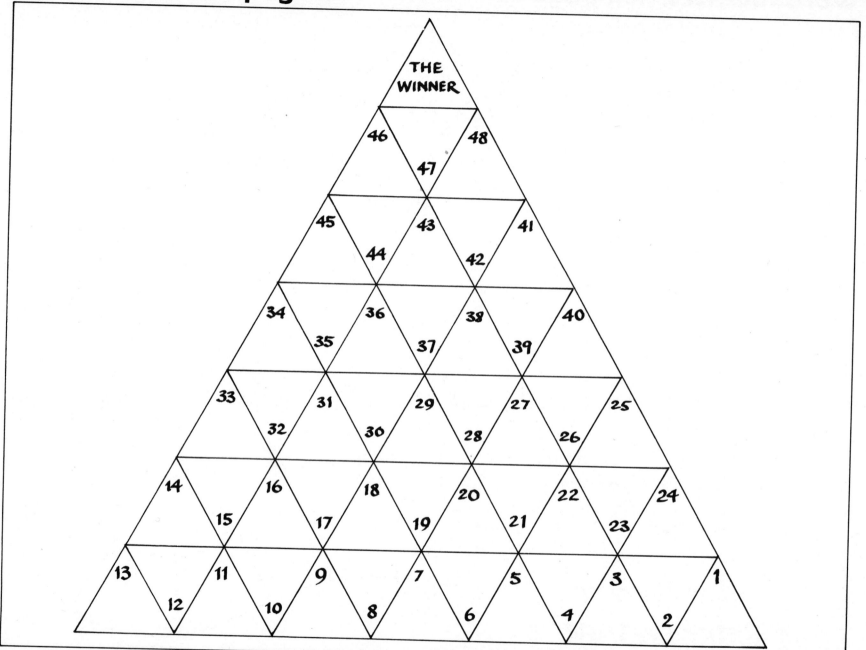

Gameboards, see page 29

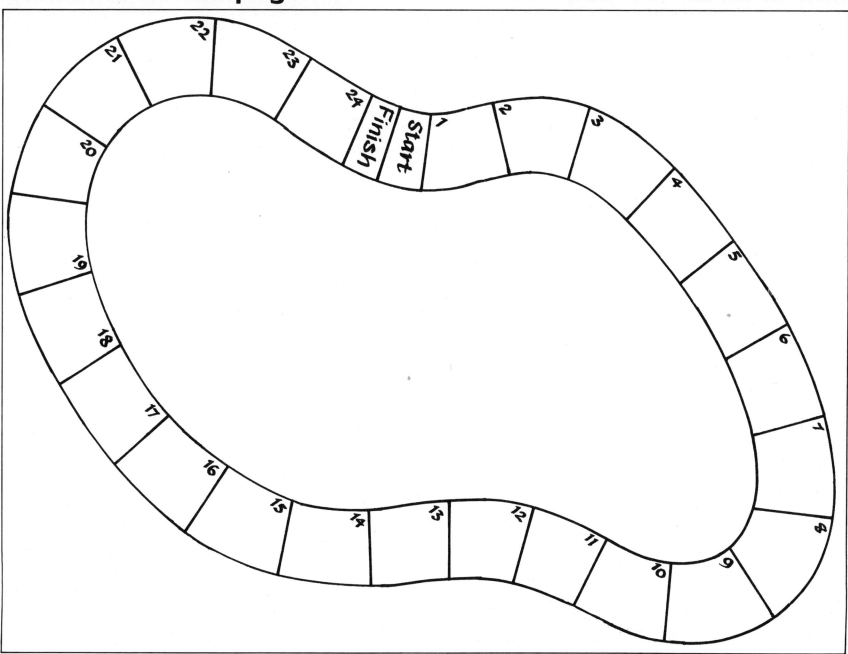

Gameboards, see page 29

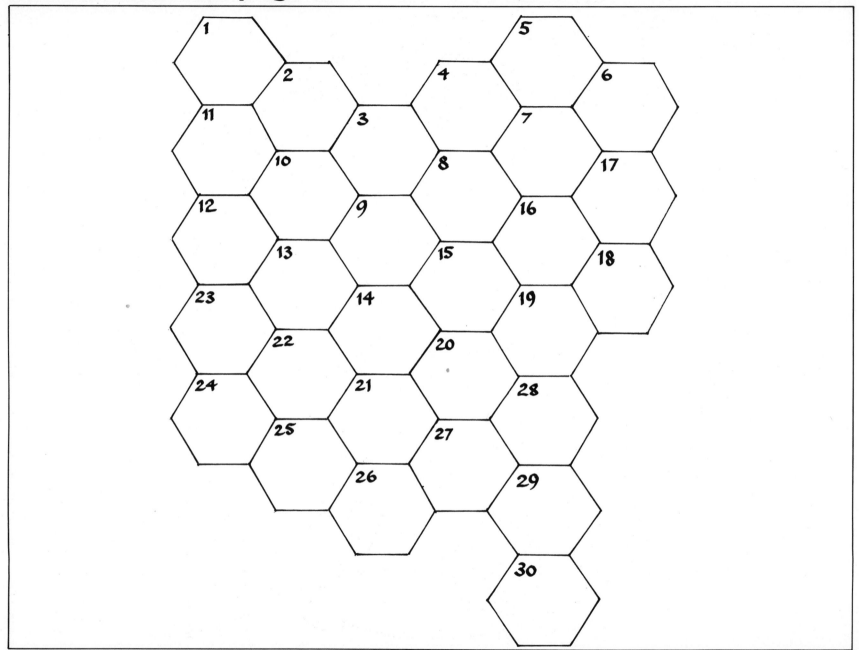

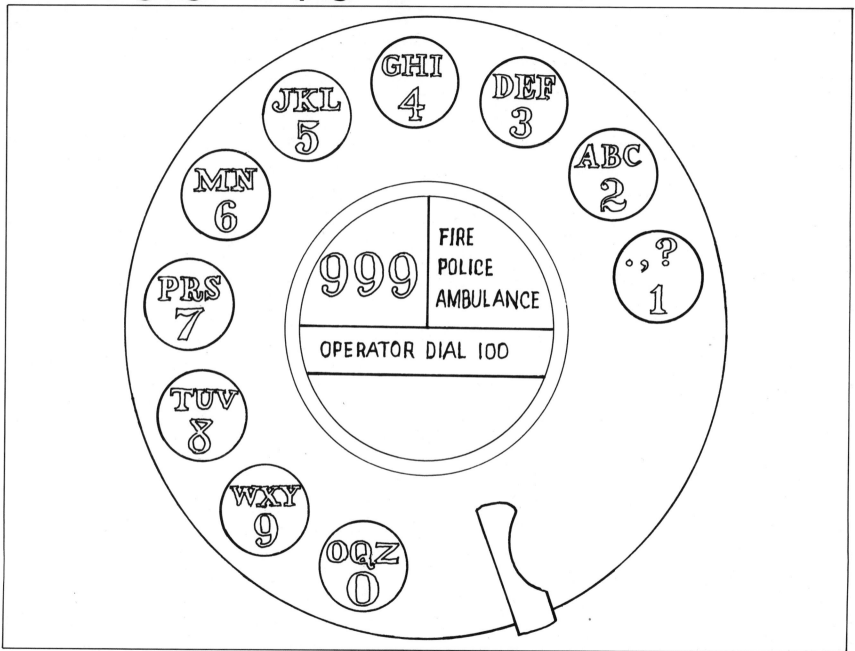

Adjective spinners, see page 66

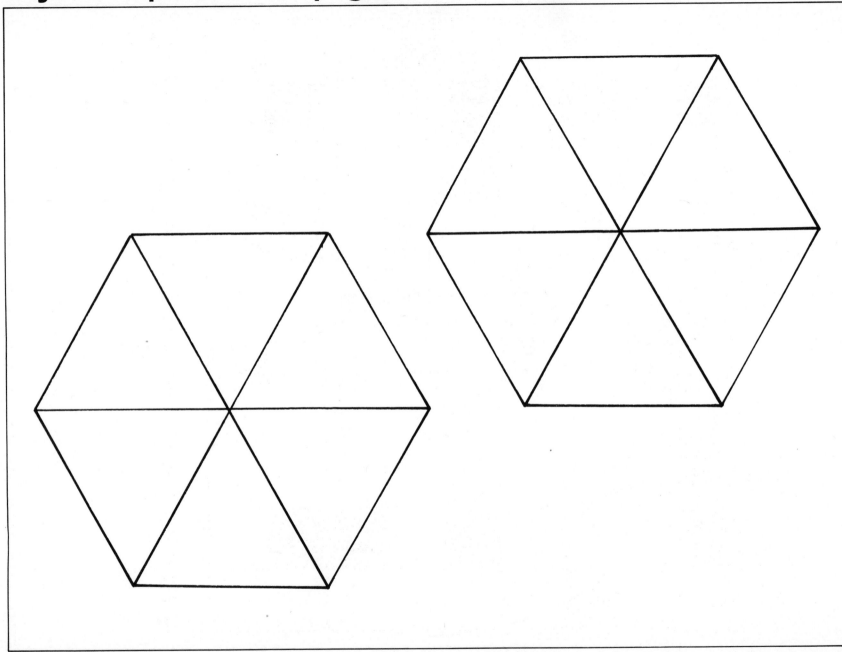

Crosswords, see page 75

Across
1.
4.
6.
7.
8.
10.
12.
13.
15.
18.
21.
22.
23.

Down
1.
2.
3.
4.
5.
9.
11.
12.
14.
16.
17.
19.
20.

Crosswords, see page 75

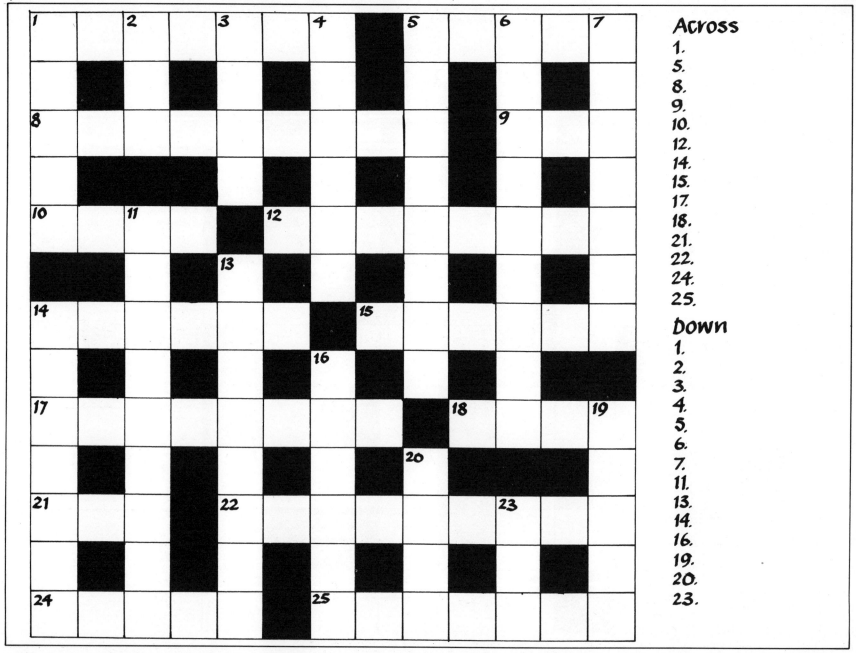

Across
1.
5.
8.
9.
10.
12.
14.
15.
17.
18.
21.
22.
24.
25.

Down
1.
2.
3.
4.
5.
6.
7.
11.
13.
14.
16.
19.
20.
23.

This page may be photocopied for use in the classroom and should not be declared in any return in respect of any photocopying licence.

Dominoes, see page 78

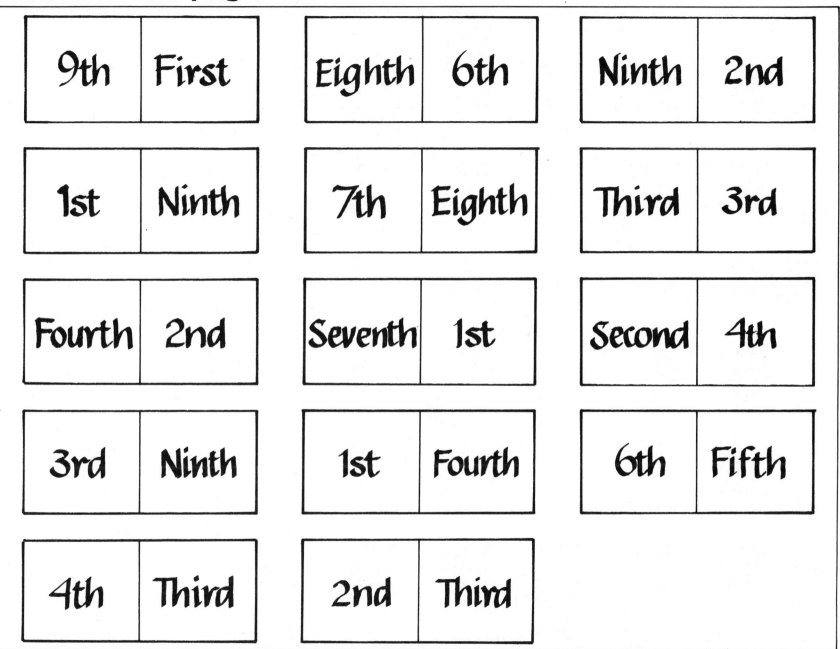

9th	First	Eighth	6th	Ninth	2nd
1st	Ninth	7th	Eighth	Third	3rd
Fourth	2nd	Seventh	1st	Second	4th
3rd	Ninth	1st	Fourth	6th	Fifth
4th	Third	2nd	Third		

Dominoes, see page 78

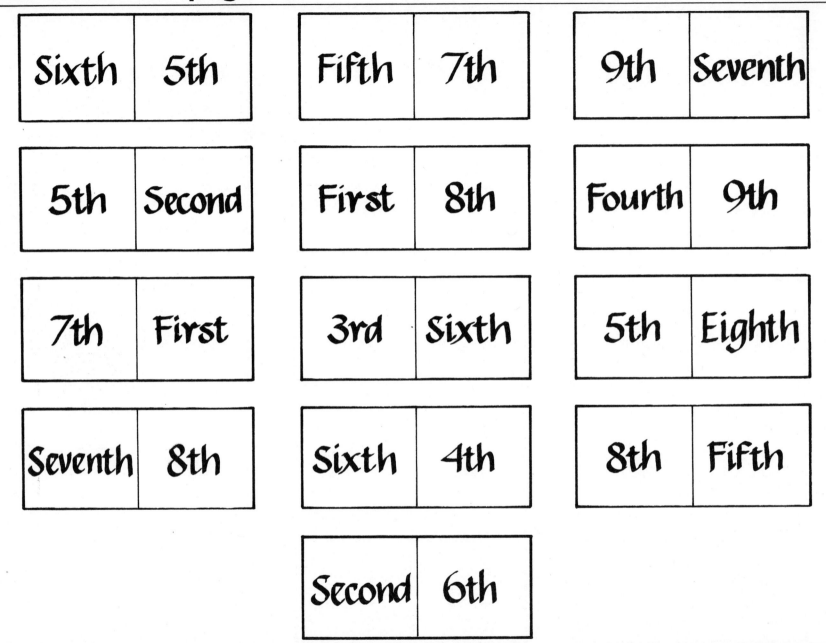

Sixth · 5th	Fifth · 7th	9th · Seventh
5th · Second	First · 8th	Fourth · 9th
7th · First	3rd · Sixth	5th · Eighth
Seventh · 8th	Sixth · 4th	8th · Fifth
	Second · 6th	

Word webs, see page 97

Word webs, see page 97

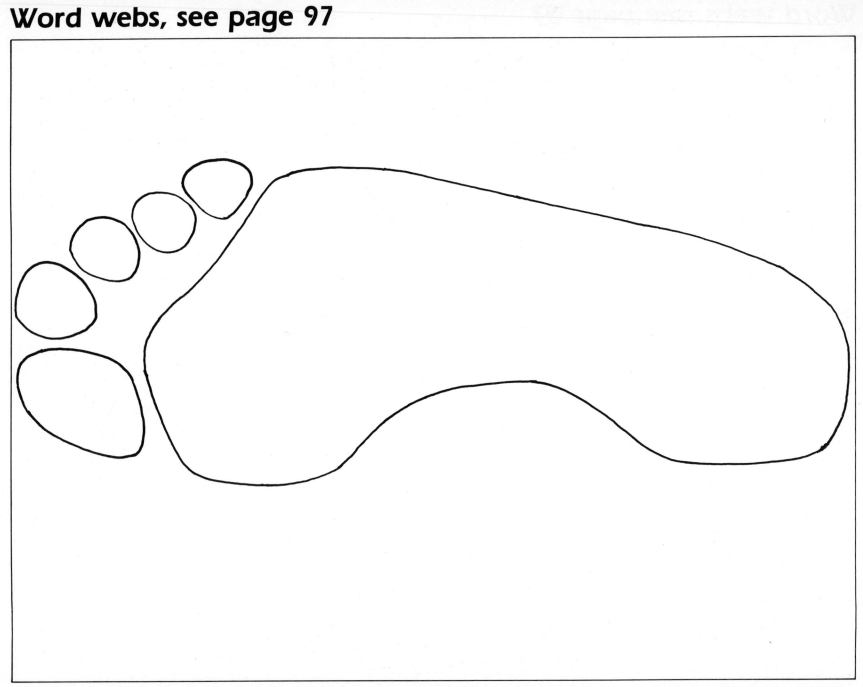

Word trees, see page 99

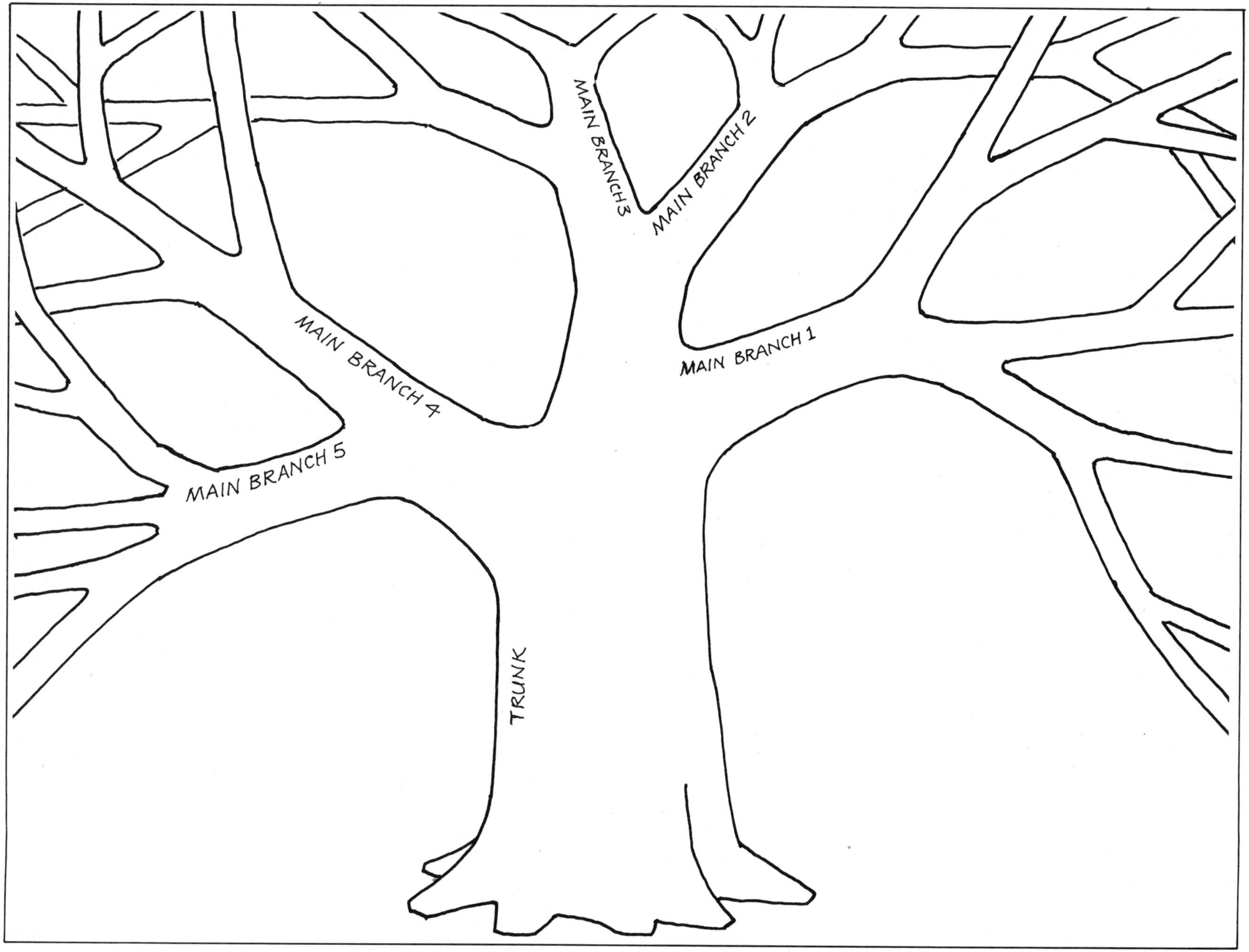
MAIN BRANCH 3
MAIN BRANCH 2
MAIN BRANCH 4
MAIN BRANCH 1
MAIN BRANCH 5
TRUNK

Resources

Some of the games in this book require the use of a dictionary or thesaurus. The following is a recommended list:

A Simplified Dictionary (Schofield and Sims).
Black's Writing Dictionary (A and C Black).
Chambers First Picture Dictionary (Cambridge University Press).
Illustrated Junior Dictionary (Heinemann Educational *op*).
Longman New Junior English Dictionary (Longman).
The Nelson Contemporary English Dictionary (Thomas Nelson).
The Oxford School Dictionary (Oxford University Press).
The Penguin Pocket English Thesaurus (Penguin Books).
The Word Hunter's Companion: A First Thesaurus (Basil Blackwell).
Young People's Thesaurus Dictionary (Ward Lock *op*).

Op Book is out of print; try libraries.

Acknowledgements

Some of the games in this book may be familiar, for many sources have been combed through, others the author has invented. We would like to specifically acknowledge the following:

'Questions and answers' and 'The exquisite corpse' from *Does It Have To Rhyme*, Sandy Brownjohn (Hodder and Stoughton).

Roll-a-gram', 'Switch-a-letter' and some examples from 'Joke names' have been adapted from items in *Word Games* by Ann and John Robson (Knight Books).

Different versions of 'Word squares' can be found in *Language Teaching Games and Contests*, W R Lee (Oxford University Press).

Permission to print the poem 'Have You Ever Seen?' by Grace Nichols from *I Like That Stuff: Poems From Many Cultures* selected by Morag Styles, has kindly been granted by Cambridge University Press.

The authors and publishers would also like to thank the children and teachers of Woodborough Woods Primary School, Nottinghamshire for playing the games and offering advice about them.

Every effort has been made to trace and acknowledge sources. If any right has been omitted, the publishers offer their apologies and will rectify this in subsequent editions following notification.

Other Scholastic books

Bright Ideas
The *Bright Ideas* books provide a wealth of resources for busy primary school teachers. There are now more than 20 titles published, providing clearly explained and illustrated ideas on topics ranging from *Spelling* and *Maths Games* to *World of Work* and *Using Books in the Classroom*. Each book contains material which can be photocopied for use in the classroom.

Teacher Handbooks
The *Teacher Handbooks* give an overview of the latest research in primary education, and show how it can be put into practice in the classroom. Covering all the core areas of the curriculum, the *Teacher Handbooks* are indispensable to the new teacher as a source of information and useful to the experienced teacher as a quick reference guide.

Management Books
The *Management Books* are designed to help teachers to organise their time, classroom and teaching more efficiently. The books deal with topical issues, such as *Parents and Schools* and organising and planning *Project Teaching*, and are written by authors with lots of practical advice and experiences to share.

International Bookshelf
The *International Bookshelf* is a selection of informative educational books available in the UK exclusively through Scholastic. Truly representative of international thinking, these books are classics in their own field.

Let's Investigate
Let's Investigate is an exciting range of photocopiable maths activity books giving open-ended investigative tasks. The series will complement and extend any exisiting maths programme. Designed to cover the 6 to 12-year-old age range these books are ideal for small group or individual work. Each book presents progressively more difficult concepts and many of the activities can be adapted for use throughout the primary school. Detailed teacher's notes outlining the objectives of each photocopiable sheet and suggesting follow-up activities have been included.

Infant Science
Infant Science, written by teachers and advisers, introduces scientific concepts in non-fiction, easy-to-understand pupil books. Illustrated in full colour, the first books in the series on *Animals* show many aspects of living things from plants, insects and birds to fish and reptiles. A comprehensive teacher's guide giving practical activities and four A2 posters are also available.

Big Books
Big Books are poster-sized books, aimed at five- to nine-year-olds, which have been specially designed so that a group of children can share a book with an adult and still have that feeling of togetherness which is so important for early readers who are building up confidence. Included in each pack is a giant-sized book, six smaller books for individual reading and teacher notes.